THE MERCIFUL LAW OF DIVINE
SYNCHRONICITY

SEQUEL to
Death, the Final Frontier

OREST STOCCO

THE MERCIFUL LAW OF DIVINE SYNCHRONICITY

Copyright © 2017 by OREST STOCCO

All rights reserved. No part of this book may be reproduced or transmitted in any form or by any means without written permission of the author.

ISBN 978-1-926442-16-7

Edited by Penny Lynn Cates
Cover Design by Penny Lynn Cates

"Synchronicity is an ever present reality for those who have eyes to see."

C. G. Jung

"The universe may very well be a living being—encouraging us to grow and evolve into our true identity. Synchronicity is the key that unlocks the greatest mystery of all time."

The Synchronicity Key
David Wilcock

Note to the Reader

While writing *The Merciful Law of Divine Synchronicity* (I was half way through Chapter 12, "The Three Circles of Life"), I was strongly nudged to go to a book signing in Chapters in Barrie, Ontario for Psychologist Teresa DeCicco's new book *Living Beyond the Five Senses*, and as serendipity would have it I met Jeanne Van Bronkhorst signing her own new book *Dreams at the Threshold* at the same table, which I read first when I got home because the subject fascinated me; and that's what inspired my book *Death, the Final Frontier* which I had to complete before I could bring my book *The Merciful Law of Divine Synchronicity* to closure, and only now do I see why.

The creative impulse has a mind of its own, and while writing Chapter 12, I got the strongest urge to stop writing this book and write a new book whose title just came to me out of the clear blue—*Death, the Final Frontier*; so I began writing and didn't stop until I finished it—and, I hasten to add, with an incredible coincidence that capped my story beautifully. Only then could I bring *The Merciful Law of Divine Synchronicity* to resolution, because the incredible coincidence that brought *Death, the Final Frontier* to closure was the perfect transition to *The Merciful Law of Divine Synchronicity*.

I didn't know it, but I had to explore my thoughts on death and dying before I could bring my relationship with the synchronicity principle to resolution. It was as though *The Merciful Law of Divine Synchronicity* called for a **prequel,** which is why I believe I was called to write *Death, the Final Frontier;* I had to provide the story that my book presupposed, which makes it my **sequel** to *Death, the Final Frontier*; and although these two books can stand alone, they are twin souls born of the same womb of my creative unconscious.

I can't help but smile to myself, because it honestly feels like my twin books were fighting to be born first, and the closer *The Merciful Law of Divine Synchronicity* got to being born first, its nascent twin soul cried out for life and I had to heed the call and write *Death, the Final Frontier*; and although my two books have their own identity, they are symbiotically related and support each other in ways that only twin souls can appreciate.

I hope you enjoy *The Merciful Law of Divine Synchronicity,* but you must read its twin soul *Death, the Final Frontier* for total literary satisfaction.

Orest Stocco
Georgian Bay, Ontario
August 25, 2016

CONTENTS

1. RANDOM CHANCE, OR DIVINE ORCHESTRATION?....................1
2. DO WE CHOOSE OUR BELIEFS, OR DO THEY CHOOSE US?........8
3. THE WAY OF SOUL 18
4. THE WISDOM OF LITERATURE 33
5. THE NAKED TRUTH UNVEILED 41
6. THE EYE OF THE NEEDLE 50
7. THE PRIVATE LANGUAGE OF THE SOUL 62
8. THE RICH YOUNG MAN'S DILEMMA 72
9. PILGRIMAGE AND PENANCE..79
10. A BREATHTAKING KIND OF NIHILISM 86
11. THE PLAYFUL SPIRIT OF SYNCHRONICITY 96
12. THE MERCIFUL MYSTERY OF HUMAN SUFFERING 104
13. THE THREE CIRCLES OF LIFE...114
14. THE ONLY WAY OUT OF LIFE IS THROUGH LIFE....................123
15. SOME REMARKABLE COINCIDENCES 128
16. A STREET CALLED STOCCO CIRCLE 134
17. THE VOICE WITHIN...143

1. RANDOM CHANCE, OR DIVINE ORCHESTRATION?

*"There is no other place to find yourself.
Now is your only context."*

I was going on twenty-four and living in Annecy, France when it happened: a soul moment so charged with energy that it changed the dynamic of my life…

I didn't know much about synchronicity. I had read the word and heard it spoken now and then, but I certainly knew about coincidences. Like most people, young and old alike, we all experience coincidences, even if we call them random chance; but sometimes the chances of something happening to us at *that* precise moment and in *that* specific way can be so outrageous that we shout *"WOW!"* in total amazement. "Can you believe it?" we ask, nonplussed. "What are the odds of that happening? Maybe a zillion to one," we answer, because that's how incredible some coincidences can be.

Such is the nature of this special kind of coincidence, which is why C. G. Jung, the eminent Swiss psychologist who discovered the "collective unconscious" and became the true founding father of modern depth psychology, had to coin a special word to identify the miraculous nature of this special kind of meaningful coincidence.

The word C. G. Jung coined for this type of coincidence was **synchronicity,** by which he meant the coming together of inner and outer events in a way that cannot be explained by the principle of cause and effect and that has a special meaning to the person who experiences it, like the coincidence I experienced one summer day while driving the 401 Freeway through Toronto when by "random chance" I saw my sister waving down to me from the Toyota pickup that her son was driving when they pulled onto the 401 alongside my vehicle from the collector lane they had taken to return to their home in Oakville.

I was driving my little Fiero sports car, and Penny and I were taking the super busy expressway through Toronto on our way to Waterloo to visit my brother Mario at his art gallery, and my sister Mary and her son were on their way home from Pearson International Airport where they had just dropped off my sister Lorette to catch her plane to Winnipeg.

I had a falling out with Mary, and instead of stopping in Oakville to visit with her as I normally would have done we were driving straight through to Waterloo, and one might say that I met my "Waterloo" when **the merciful law of divine synchronicity** orchestrated the zillion-to-one chance of my sister and her son seeing me in my little black sports car when they pulled onto the 401and frantically waving to get my attention. There was no need to pull over, because the incredible coincidence of meeting that way was a definite sign for us to make up for whatever it was that had gotten between us, and we rolled down our windows and I shouted up to her: *"I'll follow you back to Oakville!"*

That's what C. G. Jung meant by **synchronicity**, and why he had to have a new name for this special type of coincidence. But just to be clear by what he meant by this kind of miraculous happenstance of the coming together of the inner with the outer in a meaningful way (the inner being my rancor for my sister and the outer being our "chance" meeting on the 401 Freeway), the odds of our meeting in that specific place and time were so astronomical that it had to mean something special to both of us, which it certainly did; and the awe of our meeting infused us with so much of that special kind of energy that comes with synchronicity that my sister and I reconciled and resumed our normal, loving relationship.

"In a sense," writes Phil Cousineau in his book *Soul Moments,* "an experience of synchronicity is a soul moment, an electrifying experience, as sudden as a visitation by a god, a palpable inrush of grace and power, one of the defining moments in life, a sudden conviction that we might move beyond fate and realize a hint of our destiny."

The key words here are **fate** and **destiny,** the paradoxical mystery of our personal fate that we create with free will and our destined purpose encoded in our soul's DNA that has inspired me to tell my incredible story of self-reconciliation that began when I gave up my

THE MERCIFUL LAW OF DIVINE SYNCHRONICITY

promising pool hall and vending machine business in my hometown of Nipigon, Ontario in the twenty-third year of my life and decided to go to the Alpine city of Annecy, France to begin my quest to satisfy the volcanic longing in my soul for my true self.

"The universe is implicitly and explicitly of one piece," said the mystical protagonist of Glenda Green's book *Love Without End, Jesus Speaks*. *"At the point of perfect stasis between the implicit and explicit, there is a condition of hypersynchronicity, where matter, energy, space and time move into a 'no-resistance' mode of infinite potential. This is the synchronizing of matter to a 'zero point' of perfect synchronicity."*

What I experienced on the 401 with my sister was a moment of hypersynchronicity, **a miraculous moment of no-resistance of infinite potential** in which I was free to act upon or not—depending upon whether I wanted to reconcile with my older sister or not.

Whatever choice I made would have been my personal fate, and it did not matter one wit to the divine principle that had orchestrated the variables of life to bring my sister and I together in that specific moment in time and place, but so charged was that moment with awe and wonder that I *knew* I had to reconcile with my sister; and I chose to follow her to her home in Oakville where we had a tearful makeup and lovely visit.

It's out of experiences like this that after many years of writing I came to call the acausal principle of synchronicity a divine and merciful law, because it never once failed to provide me with an opportunity to reconcile my personal fate with my destined purpose, and what this means will be revealed in the course of my story which, as difficult as it may be to believe, was foretold in that soul moment of inspired writing that I experienced one snowy afternoon in my one room apartment in Annecy, France when I came in from the most despairing walk of my life and sat at my desk and wrote the following words that gave me the strength and courage I desperately needed to continue my quest for my true self:

"Steadfast and courageous is he, who having overcome woe and grief remains alone and undaunted. Alone I say, for to be otherwise would hardly seem possible for one must bear one's conscience alone. He must fight the battle and he must win the battle, odds or no odds.

He must win to establish the equilibrial tranquility of body and soul, and sooner or later he will erupt as a volcano of unlimited confidence which will purpose his life thereafter. And having given birth to such magnificence, he will no longer be alone alone, but alone in society; and he will see the mirror of his puerile grief in the eyes of his fellow man."

These words burned themselves into my soul, such was the effect they had upon me; and whenever I felt lost and lonely I quoted them to myself and continued on my journey of self-discovery. I was desperately alone in my quest for my true self, or so I thought; and it wasn't until I began to connect the dots that I realized we all have inner guidance, and I *do* now see the mirror of their puerile grief in the eyes of my fellow man today.

Which is what *The Merciful Law of Divine Synchronicity* is about, this guidance that speaks to us through signs, symbols, dreams, coincidences, and even audibly as it did to me when I hit a brick wall with my *Royal Dictum* (my edict of self-denial) and Gurdjieff's teaching and felt so dejected that I did not know where to turn. *"Why do you lie?"* the voice said to me, in my mind; and so shocking was this question to my impervious vanity that it opened up a whole new pathway of self-discovery through relentless self-awareness.

That's how I came face to face with my shadow that permeated my personality so thoroughly that I was oblivious to my inherent falseness that kept me from finding my true self; but I'm getting ahead of my story. All I meant to do was introduce the concept of **the omniscient guiding principle of life** that I came to recognize through the principle of synchronicity which I experienced enough times to convince me that we all have an inner guiding principle that is always there to help us reconcile our karmic fate with our destined purpose when we need it, even if we are not aware of it; like the time I was driving home from Winnipeg where I had gone to visit with my sister in her distressing time of need.

I had recently purchased a Hyundai Sport with a moon roof and proudly drove it to Winnipeg to comfort my sister in her marital crisis, and on my way back home to Nipigon in Northern Ontario a week later I was cruising along well over the speed limit when I spotted a large turtle in the middle of the highway a mile or so from the Ontario border, and being a New Age sensitive man I pulled over and gently picked up the turtle and carried it to the side of the road where it would be out of danger, and then I continued on my merry way very proud of myself, but my foot no less heavy.

Well, wouldn't you know it; as soon as I crossed the Ontario border I got pulled over by the OPP (Ontario Provincial Police) for speeding. But had I been less dense and truly sensitive, I would have read the sign that *the merciful law of divine synchronicity* had given me and avoided a hefty fine and loss of points on my driver's license.

I did however pay attention to the language of life several years later when I was driving my work van to Longlac for a painting contract I had picked up when a mother duck and seven or eight ducklings were crossing the highway on the twenty mile stretch between Geraldton and Longlac which I learned later was a bad place for speed traps.

Again I was driving over the speed limit, but I slowed down to a crawl when I saw the ducks which instantly reminded me of the turtle in the middle of the highway, and I waited until the mother and her ducklings had all crossed to the other side; and just as I suspected— by this time I had begun to pay more attention to signs and symbols— a mile or so down the highway I spotted an OPP cruiser hidden in a side road with a radar trap.

Both of these experiences reinforced the principle of karma. With my turtle experience I had made a choice to speed and broke the law, which had unhappy consequences; and in my experience with the ducks I slowed down and had happy consequences.

Good or bad, the choices we make have consequences, and consequences determine our karmic fate; but as I began to connect the dots with every new coincidence, I began to sense the presence of an *omniscient guiding principle* that speaks to us daily through signs and symbols, and always for our own good; but I didn't really appreciate how personal choice and karma were so intimately related until I had another experience with my little Fiero when I took Penny to the Rossport Inn for dinner one sunny spring afternoon.

I had purchased my second-hand Fiero the previous summer and had put it away for the winter, and when spring finally came I took it out and invited Penny for dinner (we were only dating then), but on our way home from the Rossport Inn I got the flashing lights from an oncoming vehicle to let me know that there was an OPP waiting up the road.

Like most drivers, I was grateful for the warning and slowed down below the speed limit, and I waved to the OPP hidden in the side road; but when I went to flash my lights to an on-coming vehicle to warn him of the radar trap down the highway I had forgotten my Fiero had hide-away lights and didn't remember which button or lever to release them, and in my panic I had my wipers wildly wiping my windshield before I found the release, but I finally managed to flash my lights to warn the oncoming vehicle; but to my horror the vehicle I had just flashed was another OPP cruiser, and he turned around and pulled me over.

"Oh shit," I said, as I waited for the officer to question me.

The officer informed me that what I did was against the law, to which I replied (after I collected myself somewhat from my embarrassment as he checked my license, ownership, and insurance), "It's common courtesy, isn't it?"

"It may be, but it's still against the law," he responded; and after letting me squirm a moment or so longer he let me off with a smirk and a warning.

Penny couldn't stop laughing, but I felt so embarrassed for all of my buffoonery in my frantic effort to warn the oncoming driver only to find out it was an OPP officer that out of my exquisite humiliation I must have left my body and ascended to a higher plane of awareness because I heard myself shouting, *"That's it! I get it! I get it!"*

"Get what?" Penny asked, taken aback by my outburst.

"I just connected the dots!" I exclaimed again.

"What dots?" Penny asked.

"It's all about karma! I had no right to interfere in that driver's karma. If that driver was meant to get a speeding ticket, I had no right to interfere. *Do you understand?"*

"No," Penny said, with confusion.

"God, it's taken me a long time to make this connection!" I exclaimed again, marveling at my epiphany. "Look, Penny; karma is all about accountability. We are responsible for our own life, for the choices we make; and if we choose to speed and get caught, that's no one's fault but our own, and we have no right to interfere in another

person's choice. *Wow!* I've known this for years, but now I just experienced it and *know* it for real!"

And that's how I gained my gnostic wisdom that awakened me to ***the omniscient guiding principle of life,*** one epiphany after another, and usually at a dear cost to my precious vanity which many years later gave birth to one of my favorite sayings: *life is a journey through vanity to humility*; and having said this, I can now get on with my story…

2. DO WE CHOOSE OUR BELIEFS, OR DO THEY CHOOSE US?

Synchronicity inspired this story...

As I waited on my coffee maker Wednesday morning *February 17, 2016* I read a feature article in one of my weekend papers, in the Toronto's *Globe & Mail* Focus section (*Saturday, February 6, 2016*); it was on the neurologist/author Dr. Oliver Sacks, by Norman Doidge, MD, and I was nudged to write a spiritual musing on our personal beliefs for my weekly blog with the title that had come to me several weeks earlier, "Do We Choose Our Beliefs Or Do They Choose Us?" An hour later at my computer with my second cup of coffee I went online to check out a quotation on synchronicity, something that Carl Jung had said but which I felt I had gotten wrong when I used it for my spiritual musing "The Eleventh Person" that I had just written the day before, and I found the quotation that Terence Mckenna had used to introduce his talk on synchronicity and corrected it in my musing, and then I came upon a short You Tube video called *Dean Radin's Extraordinary Synchronicity Story,* and I had to watch it; but as Radin told the story of his strange synchronicity (which boggled his mind but not mine), the idea struck me to write a short book on synchronicity based upon my own experiences, and my creative unconscious provided the title as well: *The Merciful Law of Divine Synchronicity,* the inspired theme of my personal story being my understanding that we are all guided by the intelligent principle of life that speaks to us by way of signs, symbols, coincidences, and synchronicities (Jung's word for **meaningful coincidences**), along with dreams and other ways that we may not be aware of but are affected by all the same, and the more I thought about this unexpected call to start a new book while in the middle of editing my novel *An Atheist, An Agnostic, and Me* the more compelled I felt to write my personal story on *the merciful law of divine synchronicity*; but why?

Synchronicity is a big subject, and it may take many years before someone cracks the code of this mysterious phenomenon that pioneering depth psychologist C. G. Jung and quantum physicist Wolfgang Pauli, winner of the 1945 Nobel Prize for his discovery of the "Exclusion Principle," studied together for many years through Pauli's dreams (*Atom and Archetype: The Pauli/Jung Letters 1932-1956*); but on a personal level we all experience coincidences that speak to us on such a deep level that one could easily believe that God choreographs our life synchronistically just to pick up our spirits and let us know that we are not alone in our journey through life, and maybe God does; but how are we to know?

This is why I believe I was called to write my story, because it just so happens (coincidental or not) that I believe that God does choreograph our life, but always in accordance with our free will; and that's the paradoxical mystery that lies at the heart of this impenetrable phenomenon that C. G. Jung called **synchronicity**...

If I may, which I *must* to provide context for my story, my spiritual musings are a form of creative self-reflection, a platypus genre of personal essay, journal/diary, and dialectical inquiry that I write for two reasons: 1, to tease out the oracle of synchronicity; and 2, to stay engaged with my creative unconscious. I post my spiritual musings on my blog first, and when I have written enough for a book, usually fifty or so, I publish them in separate volumes.

My first four volumes are *Just Going with the Flow, Old Whore Life: Exploring the Shadow Side of Karma, Stupidity Is Not a Gift of God,* and *The Armchair Guru*; and "The Eleventh Person" was my twentieth spiritual musing for my new volume which I wrote to explain why I write the kind of books that I do, like this story of my unique relationship with *the merciful law of divine synchronicity*. But just what do I mean when I say that I write for the eleventh person?

It's a metaphor. I write for the eleventh person who goes into a book store and buys the kind of books that I write that the ten people who went into the store before him/her did not even notice, let alone pick up to browse, as though the eleventh person was drawn to these kinds of books by some invisible force as I have been many times in my life; and when I finished writing "The Eleventh Person" for my blog I was called to write another spiritual musing on something that I had been waiting a long time to write but couldn't because I didn't have a point of entry that life always provides for me, which it did

February 17, 2016 when I read the feature article on the strange life of Dr. Oliver Sacks.

If it was anything specific about Dr. Sacks in Norman Doidge's feature article that offered me an opening into my spiritual musing "Do We Choose Our Beliefs or Do Our They Choose Us?" it was learning that Dr. Sacks was an atheist; but what gave me full admission into my spiritual musing was the general tone of the article that featured an overview of Dr. Sacks strange life that opened up a window onto his sensitive, but damaged soul.

Norman Doidge, a psychoanalyst as well as an MD and author of *The Brain's Way of Healing,* provided insights into Dr. Sacks life that could easily lead one to believe why Dr. Sacks called himself a "Jewish atheist." His faith in God was shaken early in life by his maltreatment at the Braefield boarding school in the Midlands, where his parents sent six year old Oliver and his brother during the Nazi bombing of London, and the cruel headmaster who beat young Oliver on the bottom so hard that it broke his cane, and he even had the temerity to send his parents a bill for the broken cane, which led Dr. Sacks to say to his assistant and close friend Kate Edgar many years later that his exile to Braefield was the major wound of his life; but one wonders if that was the major wound when we learn that young Oliver confided in his father about his sexual feelings for boys and his father told his mother, breaking his promise to young Oliver that he would not tell his mother, and his mother said to him, "You are an abomination. I wish you had never been born."

"We are all creatures of our upbringing, our cultures, our times," said Dr. Sacks, who tells us of his traumatized boyhood in his first memoir *Uncle Tungsten: Memoirs of a Chemical Boyhood* (2001); but "man is *not* fully conditioned and determined but rather determines himself whether he gives in to his conditions or stands up to them," wrote Victor E. Frankl in *Man's Search for Meaning.* "In other words, man is ultimately self-determining," adds Frankl, whose book was inspired by his harrowing experience in the Nazi concentration camps of WW II. Which only adds to the complexity of man's free will and his conditioning and why I was plagued by the question **do we choose our beliefs or do they choose us?**

When I was an altar boy serving Holy Mass for Father Muldoon in my hometown of Nipigon, Northwestern Ontario (or was it Father

Meir, I don't remember which exactly), I distinctly remember the experience I had one evening kneeling in the darkness of my bedroom in deep existential despair. I believed in God, but I needed confirmation; and I remember the spiritual anguish of holding up my right hand in the pitch darkness of my room and saying something very close, if not this very thing: *"God, I can't see you like I can't see my own hand; but I know you're there like I know my hand is there, and one day I will see you."*

So I believed in God from an early age, but how I came by this belief I can only guess; perhaps it was my Roman Catholic faith that I was born into, or maybe it was an inherent belief in God from my past lives that I didn't even know I had until I began to have past-life recollection dreams and then discovering reincarnation in Plato's Dialogues ("a doctrine uttered in secret," Socrates called it in the *Phaedo*) which began to seriously threaten the foundations of my Catholic faith which held that our immortal soul does not pre-exist our mortal life but is created in a state of original sin at the moment of our conception; and before leaving high school I fell away from the Church and became a spiritual seeker.

I've written about my spiritual quest in my memoirs *The Summoning of Noman, The Pearl of Great Price, The Lion that Swallowed Hemingway*, and *Gurdjieff Was Wrong But His Teaching Works* so I need not repeat myself (I may amplify later depending upon what my story asks of me, for such is the nature of the intelligent principle that guides the creative process); but I want to make the point that we all come into the world with an inherent belief system, and depending upon the life we choose to live we determine the ontology of our belief, and by this I mean the *being* and *non-being* nature of our personal belief system.

Obviously, the premise of this story presupposes my belief in reincarnation, which I have neither the desire nor inclination to prove to anyone because, as my one and only true teacher the mystic/philosopher George Ivanovich Gurdjieff said and which I proved for myself over and over again through personal experience, **"There is only self-initiation into the mysteries of life,"** and reincarnation is one of those mysteries; but I will explain why this is so when I have provided more context for my story.

I mention this only to show that despite how I came upon reincarnation, I began to feel suffocated by my Roman Catholic faith and suffered the unbearable anguish of feeling trapped by my own belief system; that's why I believe *the omniscient guiding principle of life* initiated me into the "doctrine uttered in secret" through my dreams in my teens and then by way of Plato's Dialogues where I was introduced to the inimitable Socrates.

I was in high school when I had four past-life recollection dreams, but I did not know they were past lives because I was unfamiliar with the principle of reincarnation; all I knew was that I was in another body in another time, and the experiences were so real and so personal—sights, sounds, smells, and feelings—that I simply *knew* it was me.

In one dream I was a poor fish monger in London, England pushing my cart yelling *"Kippers! Fillets!"* and I can still smell the stink of fish; in another dream, I experienced the excruciating painful rite of passage ritual into manhood as a North American Indian; in another dream in ancient Greece, I was a philosopher/statesman in my noble city of Athens, feeling the onerous responsibility of my privileged position; and in my fourth dream I was a black slave in southern Georgia and I tried to escape the plantation and was caught and whipped every Sunday morning in front of all the slaves to teach us all a lesson. This lifetime initiated me into the divine mystery that our soul is separate from our body, because no matter how much they whipped my body into submission I *knew* that in my soul I was free.

I must also mention that many years later when my life partner Penny Lynn and I moved from my hometown of Nipigon to Georgian Bay, South Central Ontario I met a past-life regressionist by "chance" and had seven regressions which provided all the self-initiation confirmation that I needed for the principle of reincarnation (if I needed any more, that is, which I don't believe I did; I simply wanted to have some past-life regressions for reasons which I explain in my novel *Cathedral of My Past Lives*); and this brings me to the point of this chapter: **do we choose our beliefs or do they choose us?**

Given the logic of my story thus far, obviously both; which in one of my spiritual musings I reduced to what I called "man's existential dilemma," because when we have outgrown our belief system we have a choice to suffer the agony of spiritual anguish, as I did in my youth with my Roman Catholic faith (and which many Catholics who have outgrown their faith also do because they cannot move on to another belief system that will give them more freedom), or we can explore other belief systems more suited to our spiritual needs.

Ironically however, depending upon how deeply entrenched one is in the ontology of their belief system (the *non-being* of their nature), one may need help to extricate himself from their belief system because they cannot do it on their own, and this is when *the merciful law of divine synchronicity* comes into play in one's life, as it did in mine when my philosophy studies at university could do no more for me and **serendipity** brought Gurdjieff's radical teaching of self-transformation into my life by way of P. D. Ouspensky's book *In Search of the Miraculous* that a fellow student had given me as a gift when he came back from Toronto from the Christmas break because he "felt" I had to read it.

But what prompted my fellow student to give me this book that changed the course of my life if not *the omniscient guiding principle of life*? Gurdjieff's teaching initiated me into the mystery of the secret way, which I will get into later; and it was this synchronistic experience of my desperate **inner need** for another path to my true self and the **outer experience** of being introduced to Gurdjieff's Fourth Way teaching through Ouspensky's book *In Search of the Miraculous* that began to nourish my suspicion that we are all guided through life by the intelligent principle of life; and if I may—*indeed, I must!*—let me quote my spiritual musing to put all of this together, because my spiritual musings have a way of quickening the spirit of my creative process: —

Man's Existential Dilemma

Man is mortal and one day will die. This is the reality of our situation. But in this reality lies a quandary, because man does not want to die; he wants to live forever. This is man's existential dilemma, and the subject of today's spiritual musing...

I don't know when it happened, but somewhere along the way on my journey of self-discovery I had the simple but astonishing realization that we are all limited by our own belief system, and if our belief system does not allow for self-transcendence we will suffer from the existential dilemma of our inevitable mortality, which in turn makes us anxious of our short and vulnerable life that gives rise to thoughts of our irrelevance to the cosmic scheme of things, and in righteous anger we all shout one day, *"What's the point of it all?"*

This perspective was punctuated by a series of insightful lectures on Personality that I came upon online by a clinical psychologist at the University of Toronto in which he talked about the inevitable consequences of man's existential dilemma and his best efforts to relieve the anxiety that man's oppressive dilemma gives rise to by learning how to cope with the *enantiodromiac* forces of our nature, which in his wisdom he saw as finding the right balance between the *being* and *non-being* of our mortal nature; meaning, our false shadow self and our ego personality, which he drew upon from the Taoist philosophy of Yin and Yang.

Jean Paul Sartre summed up man's existential dilemma in the following words: "I am what I am not, and I am not what I am," concluding that man is both *being* and *non-being* forever in the process of becoming, and when he dies he ceases to become and is no more. Which is why Sartre saw no exit out of man's existential dilemma, and the most that man could do was to make the best of his situation by taking moral responsibility for his life to keep the chaos of unfettered freedom at bay, which led to Sartre's most quoted words: "Man is a useless passion" who is "condemned to be free." But that wasn't good enough for me, which was another reason why I left my philosophy studies at university to find a way out of man's existential dilemma.

Finding the right balance between our *being* and *non-being* is not enough, as my own life experiences proved to me, because finding the right balance keeps one stuck on the tightrope of life that does not resolve our existential dilemma; and the only solution that I could see to resolving the quandary of our paradoxical nature was to transcend myself, which Gurdjieff's teaching of "work on oneself" helped me to do, as well as the teaching of self-transcendence encoded in Christ's sayings and parables.

But this only worked for me because I dared to embrace a belief system that provided an exit to man's existential dilemma; and herein lies our quandary, because this esoteric belief system does not come without a price, as the rich young man in one of Christ's most disturbing parables came to see.

In the Gospel of Matthew, a rich young man came up to Jesus and asked him the question: "Good Master, what good thing shall I do that I may have eternal life?"

And Jesus replied: *"If thou wilt enter into life, keep the commandments."*

The rich young man pressed Jesus and asked which commandments he should keep to gain eternal life, and Jesus replied: *"Thou shalt not murder, Thou shalt not commit adultery, Thou shalt not steal, Thou shalt not bear false witness, Honor thy father and thy mother: and, Thou shalt love thy neighbor as thyself."*

"All these things have I kept from my youth up: what lack I yet?" said the rich young man, pressing Jesus still further for the secret of eternal life.

And Jesus came to the point and bluntly spelled out the final cost of eternal life to the brazen young man: *"If thou wilt be perfect, go and sell that thou hast, and give to the poor, and thou shalt have treasure in heaven: and come and follow me."*

But when the rich young man heard what eternal life would cost him, "he went away sorrowful: for he had many possessions."

This led to one of Christ's most misunderstood sayings: *"It is easier for a camel to go through the eye of a needle, than for a rich man to enter into the kingdom of God,"* and not until one breaks the code of Christ's sayings can one see that Jesus was speaking in metaphor about the secret way to transcend ourselves by transforming the dual consciousness of our mortal nature, which I managed to do with Gurdjieff's teaching that introduced me to the transformative principles of *conscious effort* and *intentional suffering* that Jesus expressed in his most paradoxical saying, **"He that loveth his life shall lose it; and he that hateth his life in this world shall keep it unto life eternal."** As the Sufis say, one has to die before dying to be reborn to their true self.

The irony is that we are all immortal souls anyway, but we don't realize that we are immortal souls until we resolve the paradoxical nature of our *being* and *non-being*, which is what Christ's teaching was meant to help us do as he revealed to the rich young man who wasn't willing to pay the price to transcend himself; but over time Christ's teaching got so watered down that it lost its original meaning and became a hollow doctrine of salvation that absolves man of the pilgrimage and penance stage necessary for self-transcendence, and as fervent as one may be in his vain belief that the redemptive power of Jesus's death upon the cross will save him, not until one takes "salvation" into his own hands and resolves the paradoxical consciousness of his own nature will he transcend himself.

I found my true self by dying to my false self, as Jesus said I would if I kept his sayings; and at the risk of saying something that will be sure to threaten the spiritual complacency of the status quo, I did what I had to do to transcend myself by transforming the shadow side of my ego personality and making my two selves into one, which I expressed in the following words that brought resolution to Sartre's demoralizing no-exit philosophy: *"I am what I am not, and I am not what I am; I am both but neither. I am Soul."*

In Christ's teaching, I gave birth to my spiritual self. That's how I resolved the issue of my mortality and *became* my true self. But I don't expect anyone to believe me unless they have embarked upon the same journey of self-discovery, which we all must do eventually to break the cycle of life and death that keeps us trapped in our existential dilemma; and if we don't get it right in this lifetime, we will just keep coming back until we do, whether we believe in reincarnation or not.

That's the irony of our existential dilemma and life's joke upon Jean Paul Sartre, because **man is not condemned to be free as Sartre claimed us to be; he is free to be condemned by his own belief system!**

Did Dr. Oliver Sacks then choose to be an atheist, or was the choice of his atheist belief system foisted upon him by his ontology—meaning, the traumatizing experiences of his childhood which led to his loss of faith in God? And did he become so entrenched in the *non-being* of his ontology that he could not extricate himself from his atheism? Which leads to the question: how do we determine the ontology of our belief systems?

This is the core mystery of my story…

3. THE WAY OF SOUL

"Life is the secret way..."

The timing couldn't have been more perfect, which is the defining characteristic of the mysterious phenomenon of synchronicity, the **inner** and **outer** meeting in perfect harmony; this is precisely what happened yesterday morning when I was bringing the first chapter of this story to closure when Penny Lynn started, and calmly said, *"I get it. I finally get it."*

Her voice expressed her look of unexpected surprise, the same look that one gets when a light goes on in one's mind, and in one moment of euphoric insight she had finally caught the logic of the secret way of life central to all my writing.

She was sitting in my sofa reading chair next to my desk editing the proof copy of my new book *Gurdjieff Was Wrong, But His Teaching Works* as I was bringing closure to the first chapter of this story, when the cumulative force of the dialectic of the secret way of life that she was reading in the chapter "The Way of Soul" came to a head and broke through the walls of her mind and opened her up to the divine mystery of Soul, and she stopped reading and quietly said, *"I get it. I finally get it."*

I stopped writing and looked at her, but I didn't say anything for a moment or two because the look of rapture on her face was too precious to interrupt; but my curiosity got the best of me, and I finally said, "Get what?"

"Your writing. I finally get it," she replied, still astonished by her surprise.

For over twenty years Penny has been reading, editing, proofing, and publishing all of my books online except for my novel *My Unborn Child* which was published by *Savant Books* in Hawaii, but as much as she loved my writing, one of her favorites books being my novel *Tea with Grace, A Story of Synchronicity and Platonic Love*, she never really got the underlying theme of all my writing until yesterday morning while she was reading the chapter "The Way of Soul" in my memoir *Gurdjieff Was Wrong But His Teaching Works*.

Coincidentally enough (*and this is one for the books, I assure you!*), "The Way of Soul" is also the title of one of my unpublished books that pulled Carl Gustav Jung into my dreams one night because he wanted to talk with me on the secret way of Soul that he had just read about on the Other Side in my book *The Way of Soul*, and we talked for hours about the obsessive question of his life that he defined as "the alpha and omega of the self."

Jung wanted to know where the self came from and where it was going, and my book *The Way of Soul* provided him with an answer that he wanted to discuss with me, which is why he came to me in my dream because among other things dreams are also a portal to the Other Side; but my book wasn't even transcribed yet let alone published out here in the physical world, so my dream with Carl Jung came as a great surprise to me but which I made central to my novel *The Waking Dream* that is still waiting to be published.

But all of this needs some explanation before I continue with the synchronicity of Penny's euphoric realization of the secret way of life at the very moment when I was bringing closure to my first chapter with the core mystery of my story which just "happened" to be the secret way of Soul that resolves the mystery of life's meaning and purpose.

If I may then, let me provide some context for my dream with Carl Jung before returning to the delightful synchronicity that my story gave birth to with Penny yesterday morning…

I was still reeling from the explosion of consciousness that I had set free with my seven past-life regressions which I poured into my novel *Cathedral of My Past Lives*, and I had to do something with all of that unstoppable energy still pouring into me, so I decided to dictate the first of my "Soul talk" books on my drive to and from work each day, a book whose title came to me as *The Way of Soul*; and it was my intention to reveal the mystery of the secret way of Soul in my first "Soul talk" book that to my complete surprise was published on the Other Side by the time I had fished dictating my third book *The Soul of Happiness*.

I called these three books that I literally spoke into my mini tape recorder, which hung on the rear-view mirror of my van that I drove to my drywall taping and painting jobs each day, "Soul talk" books because I wanted to try a literary exercise of just letting my creative unconscious speak for itself, something akin to Carl Jung's exercise of "active imagination," but because I have already revealed all of this in my chapter "The Way of Soul" in my book *Gurdjieff Was Wrong But His Teaching Works* I'm going to go straight to the core mystery of my story which was revealed to me in my fourth past-life regression.

The inspiration for my seven past-life regressions came from Jess Stearn's book *The Search for the Soul: Psychic Lives of Taylor Caldwell* that I had read many years before I had my own regressions twelve years ago, starting on *March 6, 2004* and ending on *July 31, 2004*. Taylor Caldwell was a historical novelist with an uncanny gift for reading the Akashic records (the psychic record of all human experience believed to be recorded on one of the etheric planes of consciousness) where she got detailed material for her novels, and she was going through a severe bout of depression after her husband died and her friend and writer Jess Stearn suggested that it might help to come to terms with her husband's death if she learned they had been together in a past lifetime; hence, the record of Caldwell's past lives in Stearn's book *The Search for the Soul: Psychic Lives of Taylor Caldwell*.

I wanted to know why I was born into my family, because I just did not fit in and always considered myself a black sheep, and in my first regression I went back to my lifetime in London, England where I learned that my mother and I and all of my siblings were members of the British aristocracy, which I loathed and fled from to the new land of Americas to become a penitent fur trapper. But my father, whom I met on a ship to the Americas, was a commoner in our past lifetime, which is why my mother always treated my father like he was inferior and never good enough for her; but I explore this in my novel *Cathedral of My Past Lives*, and all I want to do here is relate my past-life regression that gave me the missing pieces to the mystery of life's essential purpose.

This was my fourth past-life regression. The other regressions revealed something about my individuating self that answered a lot of questions that haunted me in my current lifetime—like why I always felt a sexual attraction for older women growing up, why I always felt false and inauthentic, and other aspects of my life that were karmically driven by my past-life personalities; but I got the shock of my life (as did my regressionist) when in my fourth regression I went back through time to where all new souls come from—to the spiritual body of God, known by the poets and mystics as the Great Ocean of Love and Mercy!

But before relating this regression to where all new souls come from—*which will be sure to roll a few eyes because this is not something we're supposed to know!*— it would be appropriate to add that past-life regression therapy has become a mainstream healing modality made credible by such reputable people as Dr. Brian L. Weiss, who ironically enough did not even believe in reincarnation until **serendipity** initiated him into the divine mystery with one of his clients which he recounts in his book *Many Lives, Many Masters,* and Dr. Norman Shealy, the founding president of the American Holistic Medical Association.

In a You Tube video called *The Power of Past Lives,* Dr. Norman Shealy, a psychologist and neurosurgeon, makes a claim about past-life therapy that is confirmed by Past Life Therapist Dr. Morris Netherton who has done thousands of past-life regressions:

DR. SHEALY: "There is no other approach as I have experienced as effective as past-life therapy in getting people through life-long and maybe multiple lives of problems."

DR. NETHERTON: "It lets the human mind lift its boundaries and look wherever it needs to look to find solutions for whatever bothers you, and it doesn't come back. And that's the most valuable thing you can give anybody."

Given that the spirit of my creative unconscious has opened up this door for my story on *the merciful law of divine synchronicity* (I've made it a habit when writing to be guided by my creative unconscious, trusting it implicitly), I'd like to confirm what Dr. Netherton said with my own mind-boggling experience of self-discovery.

Despite myself, I became a serious seeker at an early age with a *daemonic* poem called "Noman" that I wrote in high school (which I realized later was set free by the morality play *The Summoning of Everyman* that I had read a week or so earlier), and what I sought was my lost soul which my poem alerted me to and which I creatively explored and expounded upon five decades later in my memoir *The Summoning of Noman*.

My need to find my lost soul was so great that I was willing to pay any price that was asked of me, which I did; but even after finding my lost soul I longed to solve the mystery of the secret way of life that I had awakened to with Gurdjieff's teachings and the sayings and parables of Jesus, not to mention my edict of self-denial that I called my *Royal Dictum*; that's why I believe that in my fourth past-life regression I was brought back to the Body of God where all new souls come from and must return to so we can complete our destined purpose, because in this regression *the merciful law of divine synchronicity* gave me the missing pieces that I needed to solve the final riddle of my life.

Just to be clear, my past-life regression to the Body of God where all new souls come from was an **outer response** to my **inner need** to know the mystery of the secret way of Soul, thereby making it a **synchronous experience**; but still, I had much work to do to connect the pieces that I was given in my regression with the third and vital piece of the puzzle that I had stored away in the back of my mind; and I connected all the pieces by abandoning to the creative process of my writing until I finally solved the mystery of our becoming.

So, if I may; let me relate the first two pieces of the puzzle of life that I received during my fourth past-life regression, and then I will relate the equally unbelievable third piece of the puzzle that I experienced many years earlier when I first began living Gurdjieff's remarkable teaching and had filed away in the back of my mind…

The first piece of the puzzle was going back through time all the way back to the Great Ocean of Love and Mercy where I experienced myself as an atom of God without a reflective self-consciousness. I was an embryonic soul frolicking in the pure joy and bliss of God's love, but I had no sense of self.

THE MERCIFUL LAW OF DIVINE SYNCHRONICITY

This experience lasted long enough for me to realize that I was a single atom in God's Spiritual Body of infinite atoms, but I had no self-consciousness. I had group consciousness with all the other souls, and although I was perfectly content in my joyful state of divine bliss I suddenly found myself in the world evolving through life from one eon to the next until I became a higher primate where I experienced the birth of my reflective self-consciousness.

This was **the second piece of the puzzle**. In my first primordial human lifetime I was the alpha male of a group of ten or twelve higher primates, and I dominated my clan with instinctive brute force, grunting all the time to keep my clan in check. My grunts were a show of force, and if my clan did not submit to my will I beat them savagely.

I *experienced* myself as the alpha male of my little clan, but I was *also* the distant observer from my highly evolved state of self-consciousness; and I *knew* that I did not yet have a reflective sense of self in this lifetime. But as I observed my primordial life as the alpha male power-grunting all the time to keep my clan in check, I experienced something that took me by surprise: I sensed the subtle exchange of psychic energy at the forfeiture of my clan's will-to-be as they submitted to my threatening grunts, and I can't help but feel that with this experience I solved the riddle of man's primordial instinct for power over people, because with brute force I appropriated my clan's will-to-be to nourish my psychic being—not unlike the controlling husband today who brow beats his wife and appropriates her will to grow in her own identity and pursue her own dreams just to satisfy his craven ego.

And then it happened. The more will-to-be that my clan forfeited to me out of fear of being beaten, the more will-to-be constellated in me until the concentration of the psychic energy of will-to-be reached a specific density and became aware of itself, and in that glorious moment of miraculous wonder a new "I" of God was born!

I *actually* experienced the birth of my own reflective self-consciousness, and I felt shocked and confused because I could not fathom my separateness from everything; and the rest of my life was difficult to say the least, because I cowered in confusion and lost my alpha status and was cast out into the wilds where I perished in primal loneliness and despair; but the longing in my soul to be united with the whole never left me, and from lifetime to lifetime I grew in my reflective self-consciousness until nature could evolve me no further in my own identity through karma and reincarnation and I had to take evolution into my own hands to satisfy the longing in my soul and make myself whole, which I did in my current lifetime with the help of Gurdjieff's teaching, Christ's sayings and parables, and my *Royal Dictum*.

But as illuminating as my regression to the Body of God and my first primordial human lifetime where I gave birth to my reflective self was, I still could not put the puzzle together until I made the connection writing my novel *Cathedral of My Past Lives* when I recalled the experience I had many years earlier just after taking up Gurdjieff's teaching.

This experience was **the crucial third piece to the puzzle of life** that would never have made any sense to me had I not been regressed to the Body of God where all new souls come from and experiencing the birth of my reflective self-consciousness in my first primordial human lifetime, because this final piece connected all the dots and solved the riddle of life; but I must pause for a moment before I relate this illuminating experience, because I want to quote a spiritual musing that I posted on my blog *Saturday, December 19, 2015* that presupposes my understanding of life's essential purpose which may help to explain Penny Lynn's experience of finally "getting" it: —

Man's Will to Be

"Man does not simply exist but always decides
what his existence will be, what he will become
in the next moment."

Man's Search for Meaning
Victor Frankl

Not all of my spiritual musings come to me in a synoptic vision wherein I see the whole truth of my idea and then have to work it out in the writing (and not without considerable thought and effort, I might add); some, if not most of my spiritual musing insights have to gestate in my unconscious for months and often years before they take seed and sprout in the soil of my conscious mind to grow and blossom into their full meaning, like the insight for today's spiritual musing on *man's will to be*.

This dynamic between my creative unconscious and conscious mind goes to the very heart of writing my spiritual musings, which I have to reflect upon for a moment or two before I proceed with the idea of today's spiritual musing; not to detract from my musing, but to help explain the mystery of the creative process that is central to today's spiritual musing on *man's will to be*.

In my long and painful journey of self-discovery, I came to the simple realization that **man's greatest need in life is to be what he is meant to be**. This is an *a priori* need that exists before we even come into this world, and it drives all of our other needs like our need for air, water, food, sex, and emotional succor. This need to be what we are meant to be presupposes itself because it is encoded in our soul, just like the oak tree is presupposed in the acorn seed; and our purpose in life is to grow and become what we are meant to be. This is why Carl Jung said, *"As each plant grows from a seed and becomes in the end an oak tree, so man must become what he is meant to be. He ought to get there, but most get stuck."*

The biggest, and probably most important discovery of my entire life was the realization that we do not come into this world ready-made; we have to grow into what we are meant to be, which makes *becoming* what we are meant to be the very purpose of our existence, and what we are meant to be is our essential, spiritual self.

I've already explained in my spiritual musings (and in my book *The Pearl of Great Price*) why we come into this world with an *a priori* need to be our true self, which Jesus called "the pearl of great price," but the realization that came to me in my journey of self-discovery was that to be our true self we have to *become* our true self just as the oyster has to create its pearl from a tiny mineral fragment. That is what I meant by saying that we do not come into this world ready-made; we have to "create" our true self like the oyster creates its precious pearl. Our precious pearl is our true self, the evolving identity of our essential spiritual nature.

And this is where I part company with Christianity (but not Christ's teaching that addresses the dynamic of *becoming* our true self) which contends that our immortal soul is created at the moment of human conception and is ready-made, and Buddhism also which disavows the existence of an individual autonomous self altogether, and all non-duality teachings that categorically believe that we are one Self complete unto ourselves without having to go through the pilgrimage and penance stage of *becoming* our true self as Jesus taught with his sayings and parables; and we cannot *become* our true self without participating in the creative process of our own *becoming*, which brings me back to the theme of *man's will to be.*

In effect, we have to work with our creative unconscious to *become* our true self, because this is how we grow in our spiritual nature; and even though this is a natural process that we go through despite ourselves (we are forever making decisions that involve the creative process of our unconscious mind), our inherent need to be cannot be satisfied without a strong *will to do*, because only through doing can we satisfy *our will to be.* This is why some people get "hooked" on life, like running, cycling, hiking, mountain climbing, gardening, and one's career even, because they have a voracious hunger to satisfy their *will to be* because the logic of life dictates that the more we do the more we *become* what we are meant to be.

This is how we *become* our true self through the natural process of evolution through karma and reincarnation; but—*and this is a very big but!*—we cannot satisfy the longing in our soul to be our true self through karma and reincarnation alone until we take evolution into our own hands, which we can only do with what Gurdjieff called *conscious effort* and *intentional suffering*—the Sufis call it "conscious dying," or "dying before dying," and Jesus expressed the same process of *becoming* our true self in his saying *"He that loveth his life shall lose it; and he that hateth his life in this world shall keep it unto life eternal."*

"Man must complete what nature cannot finish," said the ancient alchemists, the Gnostics of the soul; and it was this realization that man's greatest need in life is his *will to be* that added a deeper layer of meaning to the premise of Dr. Victor Frankl's book *Man's Search for Meaning* which posits that man's fundamental need in life is to know the reason for his being, which he reduced to *"man's will to meaning."*

As I said, not all of my spiritual musings come to me synoptically, they gestate in my unconscious until they are ready to take seed in my conscious mind; and when they sprout in my conscious mind my Muse will find a way to assist the seed to grow and blossom into its full meaning, as it did when quite by "chance" I came across Dr. Victor Frankl's book *Man's Search for Meaning* while looking for Joseph Campbell's *The Hero with a Thousand Faces* in my basement library this summer and which I was strongly nudged to read; and as I read *Man's Search for Meaning* the seed of today's spiritual musing sprouted as *"man's will to be"* because it completed Dr. Frankl's *"will to meaning."* And this, if I may be allowed to say so, is how the collective unconscious works through the consciousness of the individual self to help expand and raise the consciousness of humanity.

Victor Frankl was a young psychiatrist when he was taken to the concentration camps by the Nazis in WW II, and like all the prisoners in the camps he suffered many humiliating indignities in the hands of his tormentors who stripped him to his primal, naked self; but out of his unthinkable physical and mental anguish was born his existential psychology of Logotherapy ("a meaning-centered psychotherapy") which has become a remarkable healing modality for tortured and conflicted souls that suffer unbearable loss of meaning and purpose.

The seemingly senseless nature of the brutal suffering that Victor Frankl and his fellow prisoners suffered in the hands of their evil captors in the concentration camps forced him to part the veil of life and see that the prisoners who had something to live for, even if only in their own mind, found meaning in their unbearable existence; but what gave them their *will to meaning* was the inherent teleological purpose of their life that they were born with, which is *man's will to be*.

In conclusion, we have a *will to meaning* because we have a *will to be* our true self, and no amount of suffering can extinguish the holy flame of our existence.

———

This is what my fourth past-life regression opened me up to, the essential purpose of our existence which is to evolve through life to realize the consciousness of our divine nature and grow in the individuating new "I" of God; but not until I connected the third and final piece of the puzzle did I finally "get" it. That's how I solved the riddle of life.

As I experienced in my regression, all new souls come from the Body of God with no reflective self-consciousness; and as I also experienced, all new souls have to evolve through life to create a new "I" of God, which I experienced in my first primordial human lifetime; but because the natural process of evolution through karma and reincarnation cannot complete the process of realizing our divine nature, we have to take evolution into our own hands to complete what nature cannot finish. This is why *the merciful law of divine synchronicity* brought Gurdjieff's teaching into my life. My **inner need** to be my true self was met by the **outer reality** of my fellow philosophy student at university giving me the gift of Ouspensky's book *In Search of the Miraculous* that introduced me to Gurdjieff's radical teaching of "work on oneself" whose basic premise was to "create" my own soul; and the rest, as the tired old saying goes, is history. So, what was this miraculous experience that put it all together for me so I could finally "get" the big picture of life's essential purpose and meaning?

But before I relate this incredible experience, it behooves me to posit the question that puzzled C. G. Jung his whole life and the reason he came to me in my dream one night: **what is the self? And**

THE MERCIFUL LAW OF DIVINE SYNCHRONICITY

how does it come into being? This is what the third and final piece of the puzzle of life that I experienced one sunny spring day in my back yard helped me to answer.

I was living at our family home with my parents and young brother (all of my other siblings were on their own in various parts of the country), and I had come home for lunch one day when this unbelievable experience happened.

I had started my own house-painting business after dropping out of university in my third year of philosophy studies, and my working hours were flexible. It was such a beautiful spring day that after lunch I went into the back yard just to sit and relax and soak in the warm spring sun. I leaned my chair back and let my head rest on the stucco siding of our house, and I closed my eyes and just rested; and that's when the miracle happened—*I experienced the inception of life on Planet Earth!*

Whether it was a dream, a vision, or some kind of psychic experience, I simply don't know; but I do know that what I experienced proved to be the final piece to the puzzle of my life that made no sense on its own until I connected it many years later to the other two pieces of the puzzle that I experienced in my fourth past-life regression—my experience of being an atom of God without self-consciousness, and the birth of my reflective self in my first primordial human lifetime. These three pieces together gave me the big picture.

It had been a long and cold winter, as most of our Northwestern Ontario winters usually are, and I wanted to enjoy the warm spring sun that day; but when I leaned my head back and closed my eyes and let the sun warm my face, I began to feel the strangest sensation of being pulled back through time. But I didn't question the sensation and just went with it.

I felt myself being pulled back through the days, months, years, decades, centuries, millennia, and eons, further and further and further back through time; and then I experienced myself looking down on Planet Earth. But the world was not the beautiful blue orb that Carl Jung witnessed when he had his heart attack and near-death experience and left his body and found himself looking down on Planet Earth from a thousand miles above; the world that I was looking at was dull and grey and barren of all life, and gaseous vapors rose up from the earth and mixed with gaseous vapors in the sky; and that's when the miracle happened.

As the gaseous vapors from the earth mingled with the vapors in the sky they combined to create amino acids, the first building blocks of life; and as the amino acids formed I felt myself being pulled into them like a liquid poured into a container, and the moment I entered into the amino acids they became animated with the life force, and I was so startled by the experience of creating life on Planet Earth that I was instantly jolted back to the present, and I stared wide-eyed in absolute wonder and astonishment.

How was that possible? How could I have been the source of life on Planet Earth? That was preposterous. And for years I pondered this experience, but to no avail; so I simply stored it in the back of my mind and got on with my life. And then I had seven past life regressions many years later and was given the other two pieces of the puzzle in my fourth regression, but I did not connect them with my experience of the inception of life on Planet Earth until I began writing my novel *Cathedral of My Past Lives*.

I chose to write a novel on my regressions rather than a straight autobiographical story, because with a novel I had much more creative latitude to get to the truth of my remarkable experience. As Alice Munro said, "Memoir is the facts of life. Fiction is the truth of life," and as I abandoned to my creative unconscious to tell my story I engaged what Carl Jung called my "transcendent function," which is the creative principle of our becoming.

When we engage our transcendent function through the disciplined effort of creative writing (or any other discipline like painting, music, sports or whatever, given one's level of commitment), we transform the ontology of our *being* and *non-being* into the consciousness of our true self; that's how we grow in our spiritual nature, or what Gurdjieff mistakenly believed to be the "creation" of our own soul. But I can talk about this later. As I wrote *Cathedral of My Past Lives* I connected the two pieces of my fourth past-life regression with the vital third piece of the inception of life on Planet Earth, and that's when I saw the big picture and life finally made sense to me—which was what Penny Lynn "got" the other morning while reading the chapter "The Way of Soul" in my Gurdjieff book.

Soul is the vital piece to the puzzle of life, because Soul is the "I Am" consciousness of the Spiritual Body of God; and when I imbued the amino acids in my experience I animated the building blocks of life with the "I Am" consciousness of God's Spiritual Body.

It took me a long time to see that Soul is the "I Am" consciousness of Divine Spirit, which is the vital life force that the innovative writer David Wilcock has called the "Source Field" in his book *The Synchronicity Key,* about which I may talk about later because this book came into my life by way of another powerful synchronistic experience; but what I deduced as I wrote my novel *Cathedral of My Past Lives* was that Soul (the "I Am" consciousness of Divine Spirit, which is the vital force of life) has to evolve through life to realize itself as a new "I" of God; and that's when I put it all together!

When I imbued the first building blocks of life in my miraculous experience, I was a self-realized Soul already because I had evolved through life to the point of taking evolution into my own hands and realizing my true self, about which I have written in my memoirs; that's why I misperceived that I was personally responsible for the genesis of life on Planet Earth. In reality, it was the "I Am" consciousness of Soul that animated the amino acids with the intelligent principle of Divine Spirit, the vital force of life, and I was merely experiencing the inception of life on Planet Earth at the beginning of my own spiritual individuation through the evolutionary process of life—the "alpha" (genesis) of my un-self-realized self, to answer Jung's question of where the self comes from.

Soul is what we are, but not until we evolve through life and realize our divine nature through the process of **conscious individuation** by way of the secret way, which Gurdjieff's teaching awakened me to, will we "get" that life is about becoming our true self. That's why Penny answered what she did when I asked her, "Get what?"

"Life," she replied. *"I finally get it. Life is the process of evolution. Life is the way of Soul. I finally get it. Everything you write about is about the way of Soul. Now all of those quotations make sense to me. They all fit. They all make sense to me now."*

I have a habit of quoting references to the secret way of life in my writing, especially from literature which is a gold mine of spiritual wisdom; but I have expounded upon this already in my literary memoir *The Lion that Swallowed Hemingway*, and I need not get into it here. Suffice to say that Penny Lynn finally "got" my writing, and that made me very happy; and this opens me up my incredible story to the wisdom of literature…

4. THE WISDOM OF LITERATURE

"I could never imagine Sisyphus happy..."

With poetic genius, Emily Dickinson intuited the essential meaning and purpose of life, which she expressed in one of her riddling poems: —

> Adventure most unto itself
> The Soul condemned to be;
> Attended by a Single Hound—
> Its own Identity.

In a letter to his brother titled "The Vale of Soul Making," the poet John Keats also intuited the meaning and purpose of life, which helps to take the riddle out of Emily Dickinson's cryptic poem. Keats wrote to his brother: *"There may be intelligences or sparks of divinity in millions, but they are not Souls till they acquire identities, till each one is personally itself. Intelligences are atoms of perception—they know and they see and they are pure; in short, they are God. How then are Souls to be made? How then are these sparks which are God to have identity given unto them—so as even to possess a bliss peculiar to each one by individual existence? How but by the medium of a world like this?"*

What these two gifted poets intuited, I experienced with my past-life regressions and quest for my true self; and it behooves me to make conscious their intuitive genius. But to do so, I have to reveal the most excruciating experience of my life that catapulted me into my quest for my true self, an experience which awakened my "Single Hound" that pursued "Its own Identity" mercilessly through the hell of my own *non-being*.

One night after I closed down my pool hall business for the day (I was twenty-two years old at the time and operating my own pool hall and vending machine business in my hometown of Nipigon), I had a traumatizing sexual experience that shocked my conscience awake, and out of self-revulsion and guilt I divested myself of my business interests and fled to France to find my true self because the person who did what he did that night was not me. Rather, **it was me but not me**; and I vowed to solve this mystery or die trying.

When I returned from France a year later where I wrote my first novel which I called *This Petty Pace,* taken from Macbeth's famous soliloquy but which I burned for reasons that I explained in one of my memoirs, I got a job selling an intangible product called *University Scholarships of Canada*, a scholarship fund that provided for a child's higher education; but I soon realized that this path of selling was not for me, and I enrolled at Lakehead University in Thunder Bay to study philosophy; and in my second year of studies I felt myself being swept away in a sea of endless dialectics, and I panicked because I feared getting lost and drowning. That's when *the merciful law of divine synchronicity* introduced Gurdjieff's teaching into my life by way of Ouspensky's book *In Search of the Miraculous,* and I dropped out of university in the second semester of my third year and went out into the world with nothing but Gurdjieff's Fourth Way teaching to forge my own path in life.

I had to work to make a living, and after working in the bush camps for several months where I had worked in my youth I started my own house-painting business; and every day I lived my *Royal Dictum* (my edict of self-denial) and put to practice Gurdjieff's teaching of "work on oneself" to transform the consciousness of my *non-being* to "create" my own soul.

Gurdjieff believed that man is not born with an immortal soul, but with his teaching one could harness the energies of life and "create" his own soul; and despite my reservations about the fundamental premise of Gurdjieff's teaching, I knew that his path was right for me and I lived it with pathological commitment until I gave "birth" to my immortal soul one day in my mother's kitchen while she was kneading bread dough on the kitchen table.

I cannot deny the experience of my own immortal nature that I had that day in my mother's kitchen, which came to me like "a thief in the night," because from that day to the present all these many years later I no longer long to be my true self because by "working" on myself with Gurdjieff's teaching, the sayings and parables of Jesus, and my *Royal Dictum* I became what I was meant to be and realized my true "Identity." But it took a long time to make sense of my journey of self-discovery, and that's the purpose of this story…

There's an inherent wisdom to life that literature intuits, which is why we find literature so fascinating; but what this wisdom is no one can say, not even the writers. Like a wisp of an eternal but elusive truth, the wisdom of literature recedes into a mist whenever we try to grasp its meaning; and as much as we love to feast upon the wisdom of literature, one day we will see that **literature is not enough to satisfy the longing in our soul**.

That's what the gifted short story writer Katherine Mansfield realized when she told A. R. Orage, the brilliant editor/owner of London's *New Age Journal* who sold his magazine and went to France to study Gurdjieff's teaching at the Institute for the Harmonious Development of Man that Gurdjieff had established in Fontainebleau just outside Paris.

"Suppose that I could succeed in writing as well as Shakespeare," Mansfield said to Orage. "It would be lovely, but then what? There is something wanting in literary art even at its highest. Literature is not enough. The greatest literature," Mansfield explained, baring her soul, "is still only mere literature if it has not a purpose commensurate with its art. Presence or absence of purpose distinguishes literature from mere literature, and the elevation of the purpose distinguishes literature within literature. That is merely literary that has no other object than to please. Minor literature has a didactic object. But the greatest literature of all—the literature that scarcely exists—has not merely an aesthetic object, nor merely a didactic object, but, in addition, a creative object: that of subjecting its reader to a real and at the same time illuminating experience. Major literature, in short, is an initiation into truth" *(*A. R. Orage, *On Love*, pp. 38-39).

"This," wrote Orage, "was Katherine Mansfield's introduction to the Gurdjieff institute," because she knew that literature could not satisfy the desperate longing in her soul to be what she was meant to be, her "own Identity" as Dickinson intuited, and she sought Gurdjieff out to help make her whole; which is what Gurdjieff's teaching did for me by helping me make my two selves into one. And this is the mystery of my journey of self-discovery, because to find my true self I had to *become* my true self…

As Joseph Campbell tells us in his ground-breaking book *The Hero with a Thousand Faces*, the archetypal hero's journey is imbedded in all the mythologies of the world, and which David Wilcock built upon in his own ground-breaking book *The Synchronicity Key*; but I experienced the original archetypal hero's journey with my past-life regressions and my quest for my true "Identity" which I realized one day in my mother's kitchen; but good God, it took a long time to connect the dots and see the big picture that poets like Emily Dickinson and John Keats, as well as my favorite poet William Wordsworth, only intuited.

"Our birth is but a sleep and a forgetting," wrote Wordsworth in his iconic poem "Intimations of Immortality". "The Soul that rises with us, our life's Star, /Hath had elsewhere its setting, /And cometh from afar. /Not in entire forgetfulness, /And not in utter nakedness, /But trailing clouds of glory do we come /From God, who is our home."

What Wordsworth intuited with poetic genius, I experienced. In my fourth past-life regression I experienced myself as an atom in the Body of God, but I did not have a reflective self-consciousness. In short, I did not have an "I" of my own. I had Soul consciousness, but no self-consciousness; and I was sent into the world to create my own reflective self-consciousness through the evolutionary process of life, which I finally did in my first primordial human lifetime as a higher primate and which evolved in my "own Identity" with each new incarnation until my current lifetime where I realized my true self. This is what Dickinson meant by her poem: "Adventure most unto itself /The Soul condemned to be; /Attended by a Single Hound— /Its own Identity." But there's a problem here, which Katherine Mansfield discerned; and that's the problem she went to Gurdjieff to solve.

In a letter to her husband John Middleton Murry that she wrote from the Gurdjieff Institute in Fontainebleau, Mansfield bares her anguished soul: "...in the deepest sense I've always been disunited. And this which has been my 'secret sorrow' for years, has become everything to me just now. I really can't go on pretending to be one person and being another anymore, Boge. It is a living death. So I have decided to make a clean sweep of all that was 'superficial' in my past life and start again to see if I can get into that real living, simple, truthful, *full* life I dream of...***I was dying of poverty of life***" (*Gurdjieff,* by Louis Pauwels, pp.268-270, Bold italics mine). That's why she said to Orage that she had to create "a new attitude toward life and literature." Which is exactly what I did when I also realized that I was a prisoner of my own personality, and to find my true self I had to escape from myself!

This was the inspiration for a spiritual musing that I wrote for my blog, which I feel would be only too relevant to share in my story: —

The Prison of Personality

I've been waiting impatiently for several years to write this spiritual musing, but only yesterday while watching an online documentary on Vladimir Nabokov, the author of the scandalous novel *Lolita* that secured his reputation as a writer, did the idea for today's musing break through the soil of my creative unconscious into my conscious mind when Nabokov's biographer Brian Boyd said something that gave my idea enough awareness to set it free from my unconscious; but before I quote what Boyd said about Nabokov, let me go back to the ancient Greek philosopher Socrates who will provide the context for today's spiritual musing.

In Plato's dialogue the *Phaedo,* Socrates alludes to the recurring cycle of life and death (reincarnation) when he said*: "There is a doctrine uttered in secret that man is a prisoner who has no right to open the door of his prison and run away; this is a great mystery which I do not quite understand."*

Socrates said that this was a mystery he did not "quite understand," implying that he did partially understand it, which was enough to offer us a key to our prison door with his **philosophy of virtue** that he advanced every chance he got, but which was so potent in the sacred knowledge of the Soul that he threatened the status quo and was brought up on charges of sedition and condemned to exile from his beloved Athens; but Socrates chose to drink hemlock and take his own life instead. But what was this miraculous key that Socrates offered with his philosophy that would free us from our prison? And what is our prison, anyway?

"*The ancient doctrine of which I have been speaking,*" said Socrates, letting the cat out of the bag, "*affirms that they (souls) go from this to the other world (when the body dies), and return hither, and are born again. Now, if this be true, and the living come from the dead, then our souls must be in the other world, for if not, how could they be born again?*" Socrates was a bearer of the sacred knowledge of the Soul and knew how to open the prison door to the recurring cycle of life and death that our soul is trapped in with his **philosophy of virtue** that has the power to transform our personality and set us free from the prison of our mortal nature, because by living a life of virtue one purifies the consciousness of one's personality and realizes their immortal self.

"*And what is purification but the separation of the soul from the body, as I was saying before; the habit of the soul gathering and collecting herself into herself, out of all the courses of the body; the dwelling in her own place alone, as in another life, so also in this, as far as she can; the release of the soul from the chains of the body,*" said Socrates in the *Phaedo*; and the only way our prison door will open is by living a life of virtue that purifies the consciousness of our personality and sets us free from ourselves.

The irony is that we are prisoners of life because of our own ego personality that we create with each new life we fate ourselves to live by the karma we create with every choice we make; this is why Socrates said that the unexamined life is not worth living, and not until we realize that we keep ourselves prisoners to life by the kind of life we choose to live will we be in a position to open our prison door and set ourselves free. This is why the bearers of the sacred knowledge have said that man must complete what nature cannot finish, which we can only do when we learn how to create the right kind of personality that will gather and collect soul into herself and set us free.

THE MERCIFUL LAW OF DIVINE SYNCHRONICITY

This brings me back to the writer Vladimir Nabokov, who had come to the realization that he was a prisoner to his own personality but did not know how to free himself from himself because he had unwittingly trapped himself by his own belief system. In Chapter 1 of his memoir *Speak Memory*, Nabokov wrote: "The cradle rocks above an abyss, and common sense tells us our existence is but a brief crack of light between two eternities of darkness."

This life is all we have, confesses the creator of the salacious pedophile Humbert Humbert who seduces the young nymphet Lolita of her innocence to satisfy his secret pleasure, and getting the most out of his one and only life was Nabokov's mission; but, as his biographer Brian Boyd tells us, Nabokov feels that life was not enough to satisfy his voracious appetite for more life, and he became his own prisoner. In the online You Tube documentary *Nabokov: My Most Difficult Book*, Brian Boyd parts the veil and reveals Nabokov's miserable soul: —

"I think that what attracts me most about Nabokov is his delight in the richness of the world at all sorts of levels, the world of natural objects, the world of the perceptions, the world of the emotions, of thought; and yet his sense simultaneously that that is not sufficient, that he wants these to be more, and his perpetual battle to try to find more. He engaged so many experiences, but then felt the pain of not being able to relive them, as it were; they receded into the past, un-retainable. That was one kind of disappointment built into human life that he tried to battle against by various artistic strategies, and by certain metaphysical speculations, and so on. Another was the inescapable solitariness of the soul. He enjoyed very much the uniqueness of human individuality, and his own individuality for that matter; but at the same time **he felt that personality was a prison** and felt there had to be a way, he wished there could be a way of escape from that prison..."

That's what set my idea free for today's spiritual musing, because ever since I freed myself from myself I've been writing about the prison of personality, my most articulate effort being my literary memoir *The Lion that Swallowed Hemingway* that compares the life of my high school hero Ernest Hemingway, who was a tortured prisoner of his own massive ego that drove him to suicide, and my other hero Carl Gustav Jung who at the age of forty went on a quest for his lost soul and set himself free from himself by resolving his dual nature and realizing wholeness and singleness of self which was confirmed by a dream he had several days before dying.

Nature, said Gurdjieff, will only evolve man so far, and to complete what nature cannot finish we have to take evolution into our own hands, which Gurdjieff's teaching taught me how to do, as did Socrates's **philosophy of virtue** that teaches one to gather and collect soul into herself and set it free from the prison of personality; but Vladimir Nabokov, like most people that life has evolved as far as reincarnation can take them, doomed himself to remain a prisoner of his own personality by his own belief system which did not embrace the sacred wisdom of the Soul, thereby fating himself to return to live a new life in another body whose personality hopefully might be open enough to embrace the sacred wisdom of the Soul and set him free, and if I'm called upon to explore the sacred wisdom of the Soul in another musing, I will gladly do so.

———

This sacred wisdom of the Soul can be found in the wisdom of literature, as we've seen with Emily Dickinson, John Keats, and William Wordsworth—not to mention Rumi whose every poem sings in rapturous joy the sacred wisdom of the Soul; but still, this sacred wisdom remains a mystery, and taking my cue from Rumi (*"Tell it unveiled, the naked truth! The declaration's better than the secret"*), I will move on to the next chapter of my personal story on *the merciful law of divine synchronicity.*

5. THE NAKED TRUTH UNVEILED

"Man is free to be condemned..."

I respected Jean Paul Sartre when I studied philosophy at university, but I could not agree with his philosophy. Not that I understood Sartre, I had a long way to go before the logic of his dialectic revealed its limitations to me; but I was fascinated by Sartre's intellectual integrity, and I admired him for being so true to himself.

Then I "discovered" Gurdjieff at university, and his teaching opened me up to a whole new dynamic of becoming that resolved the paradoxical nature of our *being* and *non-being* that had stumped the great existential philosopher who brought his dialectic to the disconcerting conclusion that man is a useless passion condemned to be free.

"I am what I am not, and I am not what I am," said Sartre, unable to transcend himself because he had entrapped himself in the *enantiodromiac* prison of his own personality, which led millions of people so deep down the garden path that the world has yet to recover from the brilliant logic of his nihilistic no-exit philosophy; and that's when the question that had taken me through the hell of my own *non-being* found the words to express itself: **can a man be true to himself and still be inauthentic?** Aye, there's the rub...

"Why do you lie?" I heard that desperately lonely night, a simple question that under normal circumstances would not have had the irresistible power that it did over me; but because I heard that question in my own mind—*the only time I ever heard a voice in my mind I hasten to add!* —it gave me exactly what I needed to see my "false" personality.

I had taken Gurdjieff's teaching out into the world and "worked" on myself as diligently as my intelligence allowed me to, but I hit a brick wall and didn't know where to turn because I knew of no other student of Gurdjieff's teaching and had no one to talk to; and I sat in my basement bedroom of our family home wallowing in despair.

To lift my spirits, I put on Beethoven's Ninth Symphony which always lifted me to the heavens with Schiller's Ode to Joy, and if my memory serves me (*would that this be true!*) just as Beethoven brings his celestial song of joy to climatic explosion I heard a voice in my mind ask me the question, *"Why do you lie?"*

I was stunned by the question and sat bewildered waiting for more, but the music ended and I sat in anxious silence for an unbearable length of time; and then I stammered: *"Why do you lie? I don't lie. I'm a truth seeker..."*

But I could not rationalize away the ego-shattering power of that question, and it began to haunt me from day to day; that's how I sensitized myself to what Gurdjieff called my "false" personality and began to "see" my shadow, though I was not aware of the term "shadow" until I discovered C. G. Jung some time later when **serendipity** introduced me to his book *Memories, Dreams, Reflections* in the Black Unicorn bookstore in Thunder Bay.

"Man consists of two parts: *essence* and *personality*," said Gurdjieff in Ouspensky's book *In Search of the Miraculous*. "Essence in man is what is *his own*. Personality in man is what is 'not his own.' 'Not his own' means what has come from outside, what he has learned, or reflects, all traces of exterior impressions left in the memory and in the sensations, all words and movements that have been learned, all feelings created by imitation—all that is 'not his own,' all this is personality" (*In Search of the Miraculous*, p. 161).

Intellectually, I understood what Gurdjieff meant; but not until I heard the question *"why do you lie?"* in my mind did Gurdjieff open up to me, because the more attention I paid to my thoughts and feelings and behavior with everyone I dealt with daily, the more conscious I became of my own "false" personality, which in time created in me what Gurdjieff called a "center of gravity" of the same kind of **self-aware consciousness** (keeping in mind that I was practicing daily Gurdjieff's technique of *self-remembering*); and that's when *the merciful law of divine synchronicity* pulled me into Carl Jung's depth psychology that introduced me to his concept of the shadow self—the repressed dark side of our ego personality. **This is** how I came to discern the *being* (our essence) and *non-being* (our ego/shadow) of our ontology.

"Much gathers more," says the old saying, and the more I "worked" on myself with what Gurdjieff referred to as *conscious effort* and *intentional suffering*, the more my "center of gravity" grew in the **self-aware consciousness of my "work self,"** until I grew enough in "virtue" (that's what I called this special kind of consciousness) to be pulled into the secret way of Christ's teaching which he revealed in his sayings and parables, and that's when I began to "see" *the intelligent guiding principle of the secret way of life* and realized that life itself *was* the way to our true self, the path to wholeness and completeness.

But it was a dim realization that had to grow as I grew in the consciousness of my own *becoming,* because the more I "worked" on myself the more I "gathered and collected" my soul from the false consciousness of my ego/shadow personality; this is how I parted the veil of life with *conscious effort* and *intentional suffering* and grew in truth and understanding, until one day I had grown enough to shift my center of gravity from the *enantiodromiac* prison of my *being* and *non-being* (the "I" of my ego/shadow personality) into the "I" of my individuating soul self, thereby making my two selves into one, as Christ's teaching promised; and in that miraculous shift I experienced the birth of my immortal soul in my mother's kitchen one day while she was kneading bread dough on the kitchen table.

In Christ's words, I gave birth to my spiritual self that day; but it would take many years before I could conceptualize what I had experienced, which I finally did in the following spiritual musing: —

The Logic of Life

When I dropped out of university in my third year where I had gone to find answers to the imponderable question of my life *(who am I?),* I vowed to build my life upon the truth of my own experiences, and no-one else's; and as impossible as it may seem, I'm happy to say that I had experiences that answered my question to my complete satisfaction; but will anyone believe me?

It used to matter to me when I had a need to be acknowledged for what I had learned about life in my long journey of self-discovery, but over time I realized that life is an individual journey and people are going to believe what they want to believe regardless of what anyone has to say, which took a heavy burden off my mind.

But I'm a writer, and the human condition is my subject; so regardless whether anyone believes me or not, I'm going to write anyway; and this morning my Muse whispered into my ear to explore the logic of life in today's spiritual musing...

Life did not make any sense to Macbeth in Shakespeare's eponymous play. For Macbeth, life was "a tale told by an idiot full of sound and fury signifying nothing." Many people feel this way about life; but not me, despite how I felt when I wrote my first novel when I lived in France which I called *This Petty Pace* (inspired by Macbeth's soliloquy "Tomorrow, and tomorrow, and tomorrow /Creeps in this petty pace from day to day..."), I knew in the depths of my soul that life had purpose, and I was destined to find out what this purpose was. This is why I believe the merciful law of divine synchronicity pulled the enigmatic Gurdjieff into my life.

"What is the sense and significance of life on Earth and human life in particular?" asked Gurdjieff at an early age, and he was driven by his personal *daemon* to find an answer to his question, which he did after twenty years of seeking the secret knowledge hidden in mystery schools in Central Asia and the Far East; and he shared his answer with the world in his teaching that initiated me into the secret way of life that speaks to us with every experience that we have, if we but have the eyes to see.

"'The spiritual life is, at root, a matter of seeing,'" John Shea, a contemporary Catholic theologian reminds us. "'It is all of life seen from a certain perspective. It is waking, sleeping, dreaming, eating, drinking, working, loving, relaxing, recreating, walking, sitting, standing, and breathing...spirit suffuses everything; and so **the spiritual life is simply life**, wherever and whatever, seen

THE MERCIFUL LAW OF DIVINE SYNCHRONICITY

from the vantage point of spirit'" (*Spiritual Literacy, Reading the Sacred in Everyday Life,* by Frederic and Mary Ann Brussat, p. 28, Bold italics mine); and the more I "worked" on myself with Gurdjieff's teaching, the more the secret way of life revealed its logic to me. But it took many years to understand what life was telling me.

Every discipline has its own logic. Medicine, architecture, sports, painting, music, poetry, physics—whatever; each discipline has its own rationale that has been worked out over many years, forever growing in its own inherent purpose, which suggests that there is a logic to life that is implicit to everything that we do, whether we are aware of it or not. But what could this logic be?

In a word, what is the teleological purpose of life? This is the fundamental mystery of our existence— *"the sense and significance of life on Earth and human life in particular,"* which Gurdjieff answered in his Fourth Way teaching but which did not quite satisfy my irrepressible need to know who I was.

Mystics come close to revealing the teleological purpose of life, and some even spell it out as Rumi did in his poetry, which he brazenly proclaimed to the world because of his own directive: *"Tell it unveiled, the naked truth! /The declaration's better than the secret."* But even as his mystical poems, which are no less a riddle than Emily Dickinson's, declare the secret of our existence, it still remains a divine mystery; which is why Gurdjieff said that there is only self-initiation into the mysteries of life.

And that's what Gurdjieff's teaching did for me; it gave me the means to initiate myself into the purpose of our existence, and day by day the logic of life revealed itself to me until one day I connected the dots and saw the teleological purpose of life on Earth and human life in particular, which is to give birth to a new "I" of God.

As Jung said, "the purpose of an acorn seed is to become an oak tree and not a donkey." In like manner, the purpose of life on Earth and human life in particular is to grow in the consciousness of life's divine nature *("the spiritual life is simply life,"* said John Shea), and as incredible as this may be, I know this to be true because of my own experience that initiated me into the sacred mystery...

It came as a complete surprise to me and my regressionist, but in my fourth past-life regression I went back to the Body of God where all new souls come from; and if that wasn't miraculous enough, it was even more miraculous that I *knew* I was an atom of God with no self-consciousness. I had consciousness, but no reflective self-consciousness. I was one atom among an infinite number of atoms in the Body of God, and as blissful as my existence was in the Ocean of Love and Mercy, I was oblivious to my own divine nature; and in the same regression I went back to my first primordial human lifetime as a higher primate where I gave birth to a new "I" of God, and from lifetime to lifetime I grew in my own identity as far as the natural law of evolution through karma and reincarnation could take me, which compelled me in my current lifetime to take evolution into my own hands to complete what nature could not finish by giving birth to my spiritual self one fine day in my mother's kitchen while she was kneading bread dough on the kitchen table.

It was a long journey to my true self; but in the end I became what I was meant to be, taking the logic of life to its conclusion which answered my fateful question *who am I?* But I would never have realized my destined purpose had I not heeded the logic of life that spoke to me with every experience; and this is my truth which in the spirit of Rumi I have told unveiled, because I too believe that the declaration is better than the secret. As Jesus said, *"Let your light so shine before men, that they may see your good works, and glorify your Father which is in heaven."*

But I cannot bring this musing to closure until I reveal how I broke the code of the secret way, which is deeply woven into the logic of life...

THE MERCIFUL LAW OF DIVINE SYNCHRONICITY

Because I had to forge my own path in life, I was always looking for guidance for the best way to my true self; and I found guidance in Gurdjieff's teaching of "work on oneself" first, which opened me up to the guidance of life's wisdom sayings—aphorisms, dictums, maxims, proverbs, adages, axioms, epigrams, mottos and idiosyncratic personal sayings not unlike my own saying "stupidity is not a gift of God, it's entirely man-made," all of which reflect the wisdom of someone's personal experience, like the old saw "measure twice, cut once."

This is good advice for an apprentice carpenter. This saying could spare him the agony of spoiling a perfectly good piece of lumber (or marble counter top, which could be very expensive), which implies that "excellence" is the guiding wisdom of this saying—and all life wisdom sayings, for that matter. This is how I began to see the logic of life hidden in wisdom sayings; and I gathered wisdom sayings like precious gems from every source that I could find, especially books and my own life experiences.

But it wasn't until I began to see the wisdom of life hidden in the sayings of Jesus that I began to "read" the logic of life's purpose, and the only reason the sayings of Jesus opened up to me was because of the "work" I was doing on myself with Gurdjieff's teaching; so it behooves me to explain exactly what I mean by "work on oneself."

The principle behind Gurdjieff's concept of "work on oneself" lies in the secret knowledge that Gurdjieff discovered in the mystery schools he was initiated into, which revealed to him the dual nature of human consciousness—the *being* and *non-being* aspects of our nature; or what Gurdjieff called our *essence* and *personality*.

Essence is **who we are**, our *being*; and *personality* is **who we are not**, our *non-being*. And "work on oneself" is all about transforming **who we are not** into **who we are**. And the more I "worked" on myself, the more the sayings of Jesus revealed their logic to me; a logic which spelled out the secret path to our true self, like his saying, *"No man can serve two masters."*

But why is it wrong to serve two masters? What is the hidden wisdom behind this saying that Jesus admonished us to live by?

Jesus explains: if one serves two masters, he will either **"hate the one, or love the other; or else he will hold to the one, and despise the other."** And Jesus reveals the logic of this saying by adding, **"You cannot serve God and mammon."**

Without awareness of the dual consciousness of our nature, this saying would make no sense; and it doesn't for most people. By serving God, Jesus meant that we serve life, or live by values that nourish our *essential* self; and by serving mammon, Jesus meant that we serve our *personality;* and when we understand that we are both *being* (**who we are**) and *non-being* (**who we are not**), which Gurdjieff called *essence* and *personality*, this saying points us in the direction of our true self, which, as I learned many years later in my regression to the Body of God, is our divine nature.

In a word, I broke the code of life's logic which guides us to our best possible self. We all come from the Body of God as un-self-realized atoms of God, or embryonic souls if you will; and our teleological purpose in life is to grow through the process of natural evolution as far as nature can take us, and then we have to take evolution into our own hands to complete our destined purpose which is to realize our divine nature. This is the logic of life hidden in Christ's sayings and parables, and all life wisdom sayings for that matter, because they all point us to the best path to our true self regardless of what kind of path it may be because all paths lead to God eventually; but this concept needs further explanation.

Whether we believe in it or not, reincarnation is an immutable fact of life; and, as I experienced with my regression to the Body of God, all new souls come into the world to grow in the consciousness of their divine nature, which I proved by giving birth to my spiritual self with the help of Gurdjieff's teaching, life's wisdom sayings, and especially the sayings and parables of Jesus. And in my journey to my true self, I learned that **we have two destinies: one personal, and one spiritual**.

THE MERCIFUL LAW OF DIVINE SYNCHRONICITY

Our personal destiny is karmic, because we create our personal destiny by the choices we make because choice creates karma that has its own destiny; and our spiritual destiny is pre-determined because we are all atoms of God divinely encoded to become a new "I" of God. So we have a **personal destiny** that we create by the choices we make, and we have a **spiritual destiny** that is pre-determined by our divinely encoded nature. Just as an acorn seed is encoded to become an oak tree, so are we encoded to become our divine self; but our karmic destiny does not always coincide with our spiritual destiny (we can stray so far karmically that it may take lifetimes to get back on track, as my seven past-life regressions revealed to me), and **the logic of life's purpose is to reconcile our karmic destiny with our spiritual destiny,** which implies—*and this was an epiphany that gave me great comfort!*—that there is a divine intelligence to the logic of life that forever works on our behalf to realize our divine nature and which in the course of writing I finally came to call *"the omniscient guiding principle of life."*

This is the impenetrable mystery of the secret way and the logic of life's purpose as I experienced on my own incredible journey of self-discovery.

Sartre was not wrong, then; but he was only half right. Man is condemned to be free, as Sartre said; but only because man cannot reconcile the paradoxical nature of his *being* and *non-being* and make his two selves into one.

Man is free to be condemned by his own karma, which is his choice to make; but man can free himself from his own karma if he is wise enough to do so, which the rich young man in Christ's parable wasn't when he was given the key to his prison door by Jesus. And that's the irony of Jean Paul Sartre's philosophy, he wasn't willing to pay the price for eternal life because he wasn't wise enough to pass through the eye of the needle…

6. THE EYE OF THE NEEDLE

"Nothing is for nothing..."

When I stood on the breakwater that lonely day when the merciful law of divine synchronicity inspired my *Royal Dictum*, I looked up into the sky and pleaded with God to help me find my true self: *"I know that there is price to pay for everything in this world, or any world for that matter; so please God, tell me; what price truth?"*

This happened in my second year of philosophy studies at university when I began to feel myself adrift in a sea of endless speculation and feared getting lost and drowning, so I drove home to Nipigon and went for my fateful walk down the CNR railroad tracks behind our family home to the breakwater that divided the Nipigon River from our town marina.

I hadn't put my anguish into words, but in my soul I felt the rising tide of philosophical doubt, and though I drove home that weekend for my mother's sake because my father's alcoholic demons had been set free by his closet drinking, I know today that the merciful law of divine synchronicity choreographed the conditions of my life to create my *Royal Dictum* which would sever me from academia and set me free to forge my own path in life.

Inspired by the fast-flowing waters of the Nipigon River, the Preacher's words in *Ecclesiastes* (*"...all the rivers run into the sea; yet the sea is not full: unto the place from whence the rivers come, thither they return again..."*) and Sophocles' play *Oedipus Rex*, my *Royal Dictum* was my "edict" of self-denial that my unconscious gave to me in answer to my plea, and which I *must* attribute to what Emerson called the "God within," because I was coming to another fork in the road with my philosophy studies and would have to choose once again between the well-traveled road and the road less travelled by, as Robert Frost expressed man's inevitable dilemma on his journey through life in his poem "The Road Not Taken": —

Two roads diverged in a wood, and I—

THE MERCIFUL LAW OF DIVINE SYNCHRONICITY

> I took the one less travelled by,
> And that has made all the difference.

"God within" answered my question *"what price truth?* with the inspired wisdom of my "edict" of self-denial, which came to me complete in the following words that I jotted in my pocket notebook and which I called my *Royal Dictum*: *"I am like Oedipus Rex. I am going to exile myself out of my own kingdom. I embrace my becoming blindly, and I leave all of my sins behind me. I am going to go against the natural course of evolution, and each obstacle that I encounter, I will consume."*

My *Royal Dictum* was my road less travelled by, because no one in their right mind would deny themselves the pleasures of life for the rest of their life for the quixotic purpose of finding their true self, which I was willing to do; but so traumatizing was the sexual experience that shocked my conscience awake from its karmic slumber that I made a promise to myself to resolve the mystery of why I did what I did that night because I knew that the person who did what he did was not who I was.

My sexual experience was my dark secret that stoked the forge of my *becoming*, but only another person hell-bent on redeeming themselves from themselves would understand what I was willing to pay to save myself from myself, as the poet Emily Dickinson apparently did as she tells us in her cryptic poem No. XXXVIII:

> Dare you see a soul at the white heat?
>   Then crouch within the door.
> Red is the fire's common tint;
>   But when the vivid ore
>
> Has sated flame's conditions,
>   Its quivering substance plays
> Without a color but the light
>   Of unanointed blaze.
>
> Least village boasts its blacksmith,
>   Whose anvil's even din

OREST STOCCO

> Stands symbol for the finer forge
> That soundless tugs within,
>
> Refining those impatient ores
>   With hammer and with blaze,
>   Until the designated light
>   Repudiate the forge.

People, especially scholars of English Literature, scratch their head when they read Emily Dickinson's poetry; but despite how inscrutable her poems may be, they speak the sacred knowledge of the secret way that pulls the reader in, and readers in desperate need of sacred knowledge get hooked on Emily Dickinson whom the literary critic Professor Harold Bloom holds second only to William Shakespeare, his god of literature.

The key to Dickinson's poetry is her intuitive gift for the secret way, which is the sacred knowledge of how to make our two selves into one, because without this sacred knowledge one can never satisfy the longing in their soul to be all they are meant to be, which in Dickinson's poetic imagery is the "circumference" of her life (a full and complete life); and this is precisely what my *Royal Dictum* did for me, as was revealed to me symbolically a few days or so before I went for my walk to the breakwater where I created my *Royal Dictum* but which I will reveal more fully when the spirit of my story deems it necessary. (Actually, I reveal this sacred experience of the symbolic squaring of the circle in my **prequel** to this book, *Death, the Final Frontier,* in my inserted chapter "The Symbol of My Life to Be".*)*

My *Royal Dictum* was Dickinson's "finer forge" that tugged soundlessly within with every pleasure that I denied myself with the "white heat" of *conscious effort* and *intentional suffering* from the moment I stepped off the breakwater that day, starting with my package of cigarettes that I threw away to begin my exile out of the kingdom of my own senses like King Oedipus who exiled himself out of Thebes for blighting his kingdom with his unpardonable sins of patricide and incest; and for three and a half years *(and not the rest of my life as I had promised),* I forged my two selves into one with the "hammer" and the "blaze" on the anvil of my self-denial and gave birth to my true self which in one stroke of incomprehensible logic brought resolution to the paradoxical prison of my *being* and *non-being* which I expressed in one of my notebooks as my answer to Sartre's incomplete philosophy of man's *becoming*: **I am what I am not, and I am not what I am; I am both, but neither: I am Soul.**

This is how I gave away the "riches" of my ego/shadow personality and passed through the eye of the needle that Jesus spoke of in his parable of the rich young man who was looking for the key to eternal life, but not until one is granted the gift of sacred knowledge will one solve the riddle of the secret way that Emily Dickinson hermetically sealed in her poetry.

But this *is* the way of art, which Dickinson intuited with her *daemon*-driven genius; and the more she wrote the more conscious she became of the secret way, which she concealed in the obscure imagery of her poetry; but I wrote a spiritual musing for my blog to illustrate the dilemma that every writer must face when they come to the crossroads of their life and must choose the road less travelled by to satisfy the longing in their soul, and by "road less travelled by" the daring poet meant the road that calls us to our destiny: —

The Purpose of Art is Art's Purpose

I don't know why I was called to write this spiritual musing, but while working on another book this morning (*The Sign of Things to Come*) I wrote something that jumped out at me like a news bulletin from tomorrow, a hierophantic insight that was a remarkable confirmation of the theme of my new book on the sign of things to come but which called out to be explored in today's musing, an insight that falls squarely into that dreaded category of dangerous spiritual musings that always scare me.

A dangerous spiritual musing can hit so close to home that it can nick the sacred bone of one's life and come back to play nasty with me; but that, essentially, is the theme of today's musing—daring to take the risk and cross the line into the unknown territory of the creative unconscious where the objective will of the creative principle and the subjective will of the author become one willful purpose, which brings to mind those famous words by the celebrated poet of *The Wasteland*: "We shall not cease from exploration /And the end of all our exploring /Will be to arrive where we started."

From the earliest age I wanted to be a writer like my high school hero and literary mentor Ernest Hemingway, but in grade twelve I read Somerset Maugham's novel *The Razor's Edge* and was called to become a seeker like Maugham's intrepid hero Larry Darrell, and I spent many years exploring the sacred teachings of the world to find an answer to the haunting question of my life, *who am I?*

Happily, I found the answer to my question and my explorations brought me back to where I started, which was my desire to become a writer; and I wrote indefatigably to make up for all the years I had spent looking for my true self. And the more I wrote the more I learned about the art of creative writing, until one day I discovered the secret that all great writers find eventually, like the inscrutable poet Emily Dickinson, and that's the dangerous subject of today's musing...

My life partner Penny Lynn joins me in my writing room for coffee every morning, and we talk about our dreams and other things and always about the book she brings in with her to read, and it's surprising how quickly she can read a book in such a short time each morning before going to work; like *The Selected Stories of Mavis Gallant*, 887 pages long; Alice Munro's *The Love of a Good Woman*; and the book she's currently reading, John Updike's *Pigeon Feathers and Other Stories,* and we talk about her impressions of the stories and the authors.

That's how I gauge the quality of the books she reads, because I trust Penny Lynn's judgment implicitly; and her impressions of John Updike's writing confirmed Professor Bloom's indictment that Updike is "a minor novelist with a major style, hovering always near a greatness he is too shrewd or diffident to risk."

Penny loved Mavis Gallant, and even more Alice Munro's stories; but John Updike she could take or leave because his stories, though masterfully crafted and brilliantly written, did not leave a lasting impression.

"They fade away as soon as I read them. It's like he never gets to the soul of his story," Penny said to me, and I had to wonder why, because as much as I love John Updike for his brilliant style and uncanny mastery of *le mot juste* his stories faded away on me also, unlike Hemingway's stories which left a lasting impression; but when I was given the insight for today's spiritual musing, I knew why—which is why I felt compelled to explore it in today's musing; and so, once again into the breach...

Creative writing is a mystical experience. Norman Mailer called it "spooky," but he didn't' know why, and neither does any other writer that I'm aware of (except for maybe Emily Dickinson); but I resolved this mystery in my spiritual musings, because writing my musings brought to the fore the mystical element of creative writing, which proved to be *the intelligent principle of life* that guides our creative unconscious but which has also been called "God within" by Emerson and "Spirit" by Wordsworth and other poets; and herein lies the danger of today's spiritual musing, because it dares to bring God into the dynamic of the creative writing process which will be sure to raise a few literary eyebrows.

Without mincing words, then; I've come to see that *'the generous Spirit that makes the path before us always bright'* as Wordsworth tells us in his poem "Character of the Happy Warrior," which I made the ideal of my life, is the *élan vital* of life, and writers have the gift of tapping into the creative force of life with their writing. And herein lies the dilemma of the creative writer's art, because tapping into the creative force of life incurs a moral responsibility that can intimidate the most gifted writer, as it seems to have done the prodigiously talented John Updike.

Literary critic and Sterling Professor of the Humanities at Yale University, Professor Harold Bloom felt that John Updike was too shrewd or diffident to risk the greatness of his art, but he never explained why, which is what I feel I was called upon to explore in today's spiritual musing; but to do so I have to explain that the writer who does not work in willful harmony with *the intelligent guiding principle of life* will impede the flow of the creative process and damage the integrity of his art—like the novelist who controls his characters instead of letting his creative unconscious give them a life of their own so they can bring to light the archetypal truth of their story. "Art is the truth above the facts of life," said the author of *Out of Africa* Karen Blixen, which our own Nobel Laureate Alice Munroe brought closer to home with aphoristic genius in her comment "Memoir is the facts of life. Fiction is the truth of life."

I quote these eminent writers to make the point that **the inherent purpose of art is to explore the truth of life.** That's why Hemingway began every story that he wrote with the truest sentence that he knew, upon which he built the rest of his story to satisfy his literary credo to "tell it the way it was." But that's not the whole secret of Hemingway's art, because being true to the way it was does not always satisfy the creative process, as Hemingway learned when he experimented with his novel *The Green Hills of Africa,* a strait biographical account of his African safari with his second wife Pauline Pfeiffer which proved to be an artistic failure that taught Hemingway the lesson of his life that every great writer must obey: **it takes the miraculous power of imagination to lift one's writing to the lofty heights of art**.

Hemingway revealed his "secret" in his memoir *A Moveable Feast,* the final book of his life that he was working on just before taking his own life with his favorite shotgun in Ketchum, Idaho: "I was learning something from the paintings of Cezanne that made writing simple sentences far from enough to make the stories have the dimension that I was trying to put into them. I was learning very much from him, but I was not articulate enough to explain to anyone. Besides it was a secret."

That "secret" made Hemingway a great writer. After licking his wounds for the artistic failure of *The Green Hills of Africa,* the resourceful writer used the same African safari experience to write two of his best short stories, "The Short Happy Life of Francis Macomber," and my favorite Hemingway story "The Snows of Kilimanjaro," which proved to Hemingway that the miraculous power of imagination was necessary to make art, thereby confirming what Adrienne Rich said about creative writing: **"Poetry is an act of the imagination that transforms reality into a deeper perception of what is."** Hemingway gave his African safari experience to the guiding principle of his creative unconscious, and the deeper perception of his experience was revealed in his two remarkable stories that bared the wretched soul of his protagonists.

That's how art is made. But as much as I understood how art is made, I could not quite give my understanding of the secret of art the clarity that it deserved; and then *the merciful law of divine synchronicity* kicked in to assist me, which was proof yet again of *the intelligent guiding principle of life* that I had learned to trust implicitly...

I started writing this spiritual musing yesterday morning, but I had to stop because I could not take it any further; it needed "something" to bring it to resolution, and as serendipity would have it, this "something" came to me when I was nudged later in the evening to go on You Tube and watch Professor Jordan Peterson's lecture: *Jung—Personality and its Transformations*; and something Professor Peterson said about art jumped out at me, because it was *exactly* what I needed to bring resolution to my spiritual musing.

As he gave a Jungian interpretation of the movie *The Lion King* to his students, Professor Peterson inadvertently revealed that certain "something" about the creative process that I needed to bring resolution to my musing: **"Art cannot be designed for a purpose. The purpose of art is art's purpose,"** which is the secret of all great writing that I intuited to be *the intelligent guiding principle of life*.

Ironically, this is the mystical nature of the creative process that has been called spooky by Norman Mailer (and other writers, like Martin Amis), because no one understands how it works. But the psychologist Carl Jung intuited this secret in his essay "Psychology and Literature" in his book *Modern Man in Search of a Soul*: "The artist is not a person endowed with free will who seeks his own ends, but one who will allow art to realize its purpose through him. As a human being he may have moods and a will and personal aims, but as an artist he is a 'man' in a higher sense—he is 'collective man'—one who carries and shapes the unconscious, psychic life of mankind" (*Modern Man in Search of Soul*, C. G. Jung, p. 169).

Which implies that the creative process is *the intelligent guiding principle of life* that brings the truth of life into existence through the medium of the artist but which, as Hemingway and all great artists come to learn, can only be done when the artist engages the transcendent function of his imagination and transforms the reality of his experience into a deeper perception of that experience, as Hemingway did with his African safari experience when he wrote his two famous short stories.

Being aware of the mystical nature of the creative process, I engaged my own imagination to transform one of the most private experiences of my own life: *I flipped a coin to make up my mind for me.* I did this for six months with every major decision of my life for the experimental purpose of "letting go and letting God." I did this to learn to trust my gut instincts, which proved to be very effective, and twenty years later I gave this experience to my creative unconscious to work into a story, and with the power of my imagination I transformed my experience of "letting go and letting God" into a deeper perception of my experience, and the truth of my experience became my novel *The Golden Seed*; so I know how this mystical process works. But what does it really mean to say that the purpose of art is art's purpose? *What is art's purpose?*

I could explore this until the cows come home, but the short answer is that **art's purpose is to bring to light the archetypal truth of man's existence;** and when an artist imposes his will upon the will of the intelligent principle of the creative process he impedes the archetypal truth that the creative process seeks to bring to light; this separates great artists from all the rest, regardless how gifted an artist may be, like John Updike who hovered near a greatness that he was too shrewd or diffident to risk.

Which means, if the logic of art holds true as I believe it does, that the greater the truth the intelligent principle of the creative process seeks to bring to light, the greater the risk the artist will have to take to make it happen; and, as the history of art tells us, only the very few dare to risk their all for the greater truth of their art, as Hemingway did when he bared his wretched soul in "The Short Happy Life of Francis Macomber" and "The Snows of Kilimanjaro," and as Emily Dickinson did in her poetry that continues to baffle the world with the mystique of her "secret."

―――

This was my spiritual musing which I posted on my blog *January 2, 2016*, but I made a few editorial changes and revisions for narrative clarity because the point of my story is to illustrate how *the intelligent guiding principle of life* works through the individual person to bring one's karmic destiny into agreement with one's spiritual destiny, which the rich young man in Christ's parable wasn't willing to do because he wasn't ready yet to pay the price that was asked of him for the eternal life that he was seeking; but I was.

I wasn't seeking eternal life as such when my sexual experience catapulted me into my quest for my true self, but in my quest I came upon Gurdjieff's teaching whose premise was the "creation" of one's own immortal soul; and shortly after Gurdjieff came into my life by way of Ouspensky's book *In Search of the Miraculous*, I experienced something one night while trying to make sense of Gurdjieff's teaching that still makes me shudder all these many years later at the memory of the miraculous manifestation of the mandala that symbolically "squared the circle" before my eyes in the darkness of my bedroom after I threw Ouspensky's book down in disgust because

I couldn't grasp the sacred knowledge of the secret way that Gurdjieff had concealed in his seriously eclectic teaching of "work on oneself."

Gurdjieff called his teaching "esoteric Christianity," which has puzzled the Gurdjieff community from the day Gurdjieff revealed his teaching to the world; but the essential principle of the secret way in Gurdjieff's teaching of "work on oneself" can be found in Christ's parable of the rich young man; and if I may cut to the quick, I will reveal the secret way in Christ's parable to shed light on Gurdjieff's teaching of "work on oneself" that awakened me to the secret way and gave me the power to "square the circle" of my life and *become* my true self. In Gurdjieff's language, I did the impossible and "created" my own soul, and in Christ's terms I gave birth to my spiritual self; but whatever one calls it, I brought my karmic destiny into agreement with my spiritual destiny and broke the recurring karmic pattern of my life. That's how I found my true self.

So there I was, in the second semester of my second year of philosophy studies at university sharing a house with two adult students like myself and a high school supply teacher. I was in my bedroom late one night trying to make sense of Gurdjieff's teaching (I had read *In Search of the Miraculous* once already and various passages repeatedly), but I was unable to understand what he meant by "work on oneself." His teaching spoke to me, but I just didn't "get" it, and in total frustration I threw the book down and just sat and pouted.

"What's the point?" I said to myself, or something similar; and feeling sorry for myself I shut the lights out and lay on top of my bed with my hands behind my head.

I lay like this for five or ten minutes stewing in my dejection when suddenly a tiny dot of blue light appears in mid-air at the foot of my bed, and I stared nonplussed. Then the dot of blue light expands before my eyes and forms a perfect circle in the shape of a donut about three feet in diameter, and it just sits suspended in the air of my dark bedroom.

I sit up and take notice, and before my mind has a chance to react a tiny dot of yellow light appears in the circumference at the top of the circle and sits for a fraction of second, and then it grows into a thin bar of yellow light that expands inside the circumference of the donut-shaped blue circle and forms a straight line, stops, makes a right angle and forms another straight line, stops again and makes another straight line, then another right angle and straight line and joins itself at the top of the circle to form a perfect yellow square within the donut-shaped circle of blue light, and I am totally nonplussed.

I wish I could say that I made this experience up, but I didn't; it actually happened that night when I threw Ouspensky's book down because I couldn't "get" Gurdjieff's teaching of "work on oneself," and it was to take me many years before I made sense of the symbolic squaring of the circle that I witnessed that night in the darkness of my bedroom.

Shortly after this experience, perhaps that very weekend, I drove home to calm my father's demons because they were scaring my mother; so when I went for my walk to the breakwater that day I had a lot on my mind. *"What am I to do?"* I asked myself, and then I asked God what price I had to pay for truth and I created my *Royal Dictum*.

I felt adrift in my philosophy studies—not that philosophy might not have assuaged my traumatized conscience eventually; but my *daemonic* compulsion to find my true self drove me to take drastic action, and in the second semester of my third year I bit the bullet and dropped out of university to get a job and stay at home for my mother and young brother's sake, but I had my *Royal Dictum* now and Gurdjieff's teaching of "work on oneself" to guide me through the eye of the needle…

7. THE PRIVATE LANGUAGE OF THE SOUL

"There is nothing but the self and God..."

Once again, *the merciful law of divine synchronicity* stepped in as it always did whenever I was ready to move on to another path , but I had no idea that what I was getting into would be my way out of the New Age spiritual teaching that I had lived for more than thirty years after I moved on from Gurdjieff's teaching; but before I relate the story of why I wrote my novel *Healing with Padre Pio* which inspired my exit from the New Age teaching that had done all it could for me but now inhibited my spiritual growth, let me mention how *the intelligent guiding principle of life* introduced me to this teaching that I had outgrown but could not break away from because of the powerful hold it had upon my psyche.

Once I committed to my edict of self-denial on the breakwater that day, I lived my *Royal Dictum* with such passionate commitment that it opened up Gurdjieff's teaching of "work on oneself," and within three and a half years of *conscious effort* and *intentional suffering* I did the impossible and "created" my own soul as Gurdjieff promised, thereby confirming the symbolic "squaring of the circle" that I had witnessed in my bedroom that night in my second year at university, and I was ready to move on to another path that would take me deeper into my journey of self-discovery; and this new path came to me by way of a third cousin who on a "whim" one day when she came into town for a doctor's appointment dropped in to visit my mother and serendipitously introduced me to the New Age spiritual teaching that I went on to live for more than thirty years and which made me ready to *be* my own path in life, but I could not break away because of its hold upon my psyche.

It behooves me here to say something about *the intelligent guiding principle of life* that introduced me to this teaching that was borrowed, stolen, and put together from ancient spiritual sources by a very clever myth-making writer who had something to prove to the world but who was eventually proven to be a fraud by an innocent university student working on his graduate thesis many years after this teaching had become a world-wide religion of the Light and Sound of God, because it took me by surprise when I realized that *the intelligent guiding principle of life* does not recognize the morality of right and wrong; it simply *is* the way of life, and its purpose is to guide us on our journey of self-discovery by the path best suited to our needs.

For reasons which I could not then explain, I needed this teaching because it satisfied a spiritual yearning that I could not satisfy anywhere else, and I bought into this teaching completely; but I do confess, not by way of exculpating myself but because it's true, I always felt that one day I would walk away from this teaching, and that day came thirty-some years later when I was "nudged" to go for a spiritual healing which became the inspiration for my novel *Healing with Padre Pio*.

A gifted psychic medium, whom I call Angie St. Claire in my novel, was moving her home business to an office downtown in Barrie which she shared in a space with two other private businesses, and she was holding an open house that Penny and I attended because Penny had a past-life reading from this woman which healed her relationship with her deceased mother and we wanted to wish her luck on her new venture; but it so happened that Angie asked me if I wanted a complimentary reading, and I happily accepted.

Not that I had doubts about her psychic gifts, but the reading she did for me was enough to convince me that she was more than the real thing, and by "more" I mean that along with her spiritual guide she was also being guided by the Roman Catholic St. Padre Pio who came through in the reading that she did for me and said things about me that I simply had to pursue; that's what inspired my idea for a novel which became *Healing with Padre Pio*.

In St. Padre Pio I saw the perfect opportunity to grind all of my axes with Christianity, and I had many; so I asked Angie if she was willing to participate in a creative project which I would work into a novel. I had troubling issues with my Roman Catholic faith, which went back to my past lifetime in Paris, France in the mid-17th Century, and knowing that St. Padre Pio had been credited with many miraculous healings throughout the world, I asked him if he would work with me to help resolve my deep-seated issues with Christianity, and he gladly and joyfully accepted, and I say "joyfully" because it gave him great joy to help people.

And as I read the ten or twelve biographies on his life, I had ten one and a half hour spiritual healing sessions with the psychic medium who channeled St. Padre Pio, one session per month which I taped and transcribed for my novel; and in the process not only did St. Padre Pio, whom I simply called Padre because it felt like we had been friends forever (he was a fellow countryman born in the village of Pietrelcina in the province of Benevento north of where I was born in the village of Panettieri, Calabria), resolve my issues with Christianity, he slew my spiritual vanity which had crystallized as I lived that "elitist" New Age teaching of the Light and Sound of God with the sanctifying grace of his patience, compassion, and humility and freed me from the psychic hold that my spiritual path had upon me and which I wrote about in my book *The Pearl of Great Price.*

In one of my spiritual healing sessions Padre Pio suggested that I read a book called *Love without End, Jesus Speaks* by Glenda Green, the true story of how the artist got to paint the portrait of Jesus who appeared to her over a period of months, and which I read with joyful enthusiasm before my next session because Jesus spoke to what he did not reveal in the Gospels of Matthew, Mark, Luke, and John; but I also picked up her second book *The Keys of Jeshua* in which Jeshua (Jesus) said something in Chapter 1, "Love Is Who You Are," that summed up everything that spoke to my own journey of self-discovery: **"...there is nothing but the self and God."**

Finally, the period at the end of the sentence of my life-weary quest; and that simple truth by Jesus broke the psychic hold that that New Age spiritual teaching with its fantastic mythical history had upon me (*I guess if you want to fool the public, the bigger the lie the easier it will be for the public to buy into!*), and I walked away from this spiritual path with great sadness in my heart but no rancor, which I wrote about in a spiritual musing that I posted on my blog on *Saturday, May 30, 2015:* —

THE MERCIFUL LAW OF DIVINE SYNCHRONICITY

My Parable of the Packages

"By indirections find directions out."
Hamlet Act 2, Scene 1
Shakespeare

Truth comes in many packages, and no two packages are the same. Some packages are plain and simple, covered in brown paper and tied with plain white string, and others are wrapped in gold or silver paper and tied with elaborate ribbons of many colours; but the truth inside the packages is all the same. This is my parable of the packages, and today's spiritual musing...

I became a truth seeker from the day I read Somerset Maugham's novel *The Razor's Edge* in high school. That was a lifetime ago. Recently I was online doing research on the alluring New Age spiritual teaching of the Light and Sound of God that I lived for many years when I came to the end of my study of another teaching that had opened up the secret way of life to me, Gurdjieff's Fourth Way teaching of "work on oneself," and I chanced upon the movie *The Razor's Edge* online and had to watch it again just to see how far I had come in my long journey of self-discovery.

I had a heavy heart from my disconcerting research on the inveterate truth-seeking founder of the New Age teaching that had come to me serendipitously to expand my spiritual horizons when I had to move on from Gurdjieff's teaching because it had done all it could for me, and I watched *The Razor's Edge* with such fierce objectivity that it made Maugham's hero Larry Darrell's quest for truth seem almost shallow and frivolous; but I enjoyed it all the same, because it brought back memories of the heady excitement of my own spiritual quest for my true self.

I had seen the movie long ago, the Tyrone Power version and not the Bill Murray fiasco that lacked substance and credibility; but after all these many years and my online research on the origin of Maugham's hero Larry Darrell I came away from the story skeptical of the author's artistic intentions, which I now saw as clever pretentions not unlike those of the founder of the New Age spiritual teaching of the Light and Sound of God who was not what he purported to be. He was a real person who fabricated his own fictional spiritual identity while Larry Darrell was a fictional person whom Maugham fabricated for his story: two separate packages with their own truth that in my profound naiveté I bought into respectively.

Larry Darrell was the central character of *The Razor's Edge*, and he walked away from his fiancé and conventional life to go into the world to seek an answer to life's meaning and purpose. He was still a young man with his life ahead of him, but he had an experience during the war that called him to a higher purpose than marriage and family life, and he was bound by his conscience to be true to his calling.

Larry was a fighter pilot in WW I, and during a "dogfight" his pilot friend sacrificed his life to save Larry's; and Larry had to know why he was spared and his friend had to die. That's why he became a truth seeker whose story the internationally famous author William Somerset Maugham had to write; but it's in the way he packaged Larry Darrell's story that interested me all these many years later.

When I read *The Razor's Edge* in high school I took Maugham at his word that his story was all true. "I have invented nothing," he tells us early in his story; and I even made inquiries through a magazine advertisement with an agency that hunted down lost books to see if they could locate the book that Maugham's fictional hero Larry Darrell had written (*which only revealed my incredible naiveté*); but Maugham gave his novel such credibility by inserting himself into the story that I foolishly believed his story to be biographically true. As he said, "I have invented nothing."

That's how clever the author was in packaging Larry Darrell's care-free bohemian life and romantic quest for truth, but he was not half as clever as the modern day founder of the New Age spiritual teachings of the Light and Sound of God; this fearless truth-seeking American writer with a charming southern accent invented a whole new lineage of Spiritual Masters and packaged his own life and plagiarized spiritual teachings with a highly seductive but fraudulent mythology that gave innocent seekers like myself what we were looking for, and much more. Which begs the question: *does packaging damage the truth inside the package?*

I was born into a southern Italian Roman Catholic family, and I embraced the package of my Roman Catholic faith without question. I was an altar boy, and I even considered becoming a priest one day; but all through high school I suffered from what can only be called spiritual claustrophobia because my faith constrained me, and when I read *The Razor's Edge* in high school I was called to a higher purpose and became a truth seeker like Larry Darrell. And I discovered reincarnation.

First in my dreams with four past-life recollection dreams of living in another body in another time and place, and later in Plato's Dialogues and the Edgar Cayce literature; and I walked away from my Roman Catholic faith which I learned many years later was a beautifully wrapped package of the true teachings of the secret way that Jesus gave to the world in his sayings and parables; but it took many years before I resolved my issues with my Catholic faith and Jesus Christ's true teaching.

If reincarnation is a fact of life which I came to believe, then our immortal soul is not created at the moment of human conception as Christianity would have us believe; we pre-exist our mortal human body and return to live life over again to grow in our divine nature until we have grown enough to break the cycle of life and death and are called to a higher purpose, like my fictional hero Larry Darrell and all truth seekers who are called to their destined purpose; but does this make the enticing teaching of salvation through Jesus Christ's death upon the cross moot?

At first I thought it did, until I explored the contents of the package and learned the true meaning of Jesus Christ's teaching, and I ceased to harbor resentment for my Roman Catholic faith that denied me the truth of the secret way found in the sayings and parables of Jesus inside the Christian package, because my Roman Catholic faith had instilled in me a conscience and fine sense of moral purpose, and inside the packaged lie of Christianity can be found the sacred truth of our divine nature.

So I was well prepared for what I learned online about the clever founder of the New Age spiritual teaching of the Light and Sound of God that I embraced without question, and I harbor no resentment for the founder and this fabricated teaching as many members who walked away from it have because they were disillusioned by the monumental lies that he had perpetrated upon them.

The founder of this teaching, who once worked for L. Ron Hubbard, the founder of Scientology, was proven to be a clever fabricator who embroidered a mythical story which he plagiarized from authentic spiritual sources, a story so brilliantly woven that it took the innocence of an intrepid twenty year-old graduate student doing research for a term paper to discover the false coins that he had mingled with the true coins inside the golden-papered package of his spiritual teaching that he released to the modern world in the soul-searching, flower-powered 1960s; but rather than come clean with its fraudulent history, the current third leader of this spiritual teaching continues to cling to the embroidered story perpetrated by its fraudulent myth-making founder, and this mars the package with an ugly stain that gravely impairs the integrity of this purloined ancient teaching, so much so that I had to leave.

The fat lady stopped singing, and I walked away from this teaching when I brought closure to my book *The Pearl of Great Price* that told the story of my quest for the most precious treasure in the world, and I comforted myself with the axiom that *art is the truth above the facts of life* because I finally understood why Somerset Maugham, who besides fanning the flame of my calling to become a truth seeker also taught me a secret on the art of story writing, did what he did to get to the

THE MERCIFUL LAW OF DIVINE SYNCHRONICITY

truth of his story above the facts of his hero Larry Darrell's life and why the clever founder of that New Age teaching fabricated his spellbinding story to bring the true coins of ancient spiritual teachings to a spiritually famished world; both my fictional truth-seeking hero Larry Darrell and the mythmaking creator of the New Age teaching of the Light and Sound of God satisfied the longing in my soul for wholeness and completeness; and as bittersweet as it may be, this is my parable of the packages, and I hold no rancor for these clever arch deceivers who played me for a fool because this is exactly what I needed to grow in my own identity and *be* my own path in life .

"The path is very difficult," said Carl Jung to Miguel Serrano in his book *C. G. Jung and Hermann Hesse, A Record of Two Friendships*. Serrano visited Jung at his home in Kusnacht and he tried to explain to Serrano the mystery of the mystical marriage that was the goal of the secret way that he had intuited in his consuming studies of ancient Gnostic and alchemical texts and which was **serendipitously** confirmed by the Taoist text *The Secret of the Golden Flower* that his friend Richard Wilhelm had sent to him with a request to write a commentary, but being near the end of his life and not in good health when Serrano visited him, Jung was deeply reflective, "as though he were talking to himself," said Serrano: "Somewhere there was once a Flower, a Stone, a Crystal, a Queen, a King, a Palace, a Lover and his Beloved, and this was long ago, on an Island somewhere in the ocean five thousand years ago...Such is Love, the Mystic Flower of the Soul. This is the center, the Self..."
"Jung spoke as though he were in a trance," Serrano wrote. 'Nobody understands what I mean. Only a poet could begin to understand," said Jung, leaving Serrano perplexed by Jung's deep reflections on the path of the secret way to one's divine center; but this is the mystery central to Jung's psychology of individuation that opened up to me because I too had intuited the secret way as I lived Gurdjieff's teaching, my *Royal Dictum*, and the wisdom sayings of Jesus that transformed my inner and outer self into one self neither

male nor female with no hypocrisy, and I felt such kinship with Carl Jung that it should not have come as a surprise when he visited me in my dream to discuss my book *The Way of Soul* that was not even transcribed yet let alone published on this side of the great divide.

I knew something about Carl Jung that no one else did, and that was the impenetrable mystery of the secret way that Jung began to explore when he broke from his mentor and colleague Sigmund Freud to blaze his own trail in life, which led to his "confrontation with the unconscious" that he recorded in six black notebooks that he later transcribed into his iconic *Red Book* which Jung confessed to being the source material for his psychology.

Like the poet Emily Dickinson and every soul that intuits the secret way of the *intelligent guiding principle of life*, Carl Jung became an intuitive *knower* of the secret way, and like Emily Dickinson who couched *her* sacred knowledge of the secret way in cryptic poetic imagery so too did Carl Jung couch *his* sacred knowledge of the secret way in his arcane psychology of individuation; that's why one can sense a deep and mystifying message in Carl Jung's writing just as one can sense a deep and mystifying message in Emily Dickinson's poetry, and although it's the same message of the secret way it is always revealed through the private language of the individual soul because, as Jesus said to Glenda Green, *"there is nothing but the self and God."* But this needs some explanation.

Given the logic of my quest for my true self, as challenging as it may be, I can in all confidence say that **all souls come from the Body of God as un-self-realized atoms of God, and our purpose in life is to evolve through the natural process of evolution for the destined purpose of realizing our divine nature, which we can only do through the medium of a reflective self-consciousness**. I experienced being an atom of God without a reflective "I", and I also experienced the birth of my reflective "I" in my first primordial human lifetime as the alpha male of a small group of higher primates, and I grew in the consciousness of my reflective "I" through karma and reincarnation until nature could evolve me no further and I was called to my destined purpose in my current lifetime to complete what nature could not finish with Gurdjieff's teaching, just as Emily Dickinson was called to her destined purpose through her path of poetry and Carl Jung through his psychology of individuation—as is every person called to their own process of individuation.

"The real history of the world seems to be the progressive incarnation of the deity," wrote Jung in one of his private letters, intuiting the destined purpose of life on earth being the birth to a new "I" of God through the natural process of evolution; and when life has evolved an individual soul as far as it can through karma and reincarnation, one is called by *the intelligent guiding principle of life* to take evolution into their own hand to complete what nature cannot finish, as Emily Dickinson was called through her *daemonic* genius for poetry: "Adventure most unto itself /The Soul condemned to be; / Attended by a Single Hound— / Its own Identity," and as Carl Jung was called by his passionate commitment to his profession, as he tells us in his commentary to *The Secret of the Golden Flower*: "I was completely ignorant of Chinese philosophy, and only later did my professional experience show me that in my technique I had been unconsciously led along that secret way which has been the preoccupation of the best minds of the Far East for centuries."

"Life is a journey of the self," St. Padre Pio said to me in one of my spiritual healing sessions through the psychic medium who channeled him, which nicely complimented my own saying that I had distilled out of my own life experiences long before I wrote *Healing with Padre Pio*: **"Life is an individual journey."** And together these two sayings reflected the divine wisdom of Christ's saying **"…there is nothing but the self and God."**

Which confirms the divine logic of the secret way that only through the realization of our own identity will we complete our destined purpose to wholeness and completeness and return back home to God where we came from, as Jesus implied to the rich young man in one of his most misunderstood parables, which I will explore in my next chapter…

8. THE RICH YOUNG MAN'S DILEMMA

"The problem of resistance to understanding..."

The French artist Paul Gaugin created a painting in Tahiti in 1897 and inscribed in the upper left corner: *"Where do we come from? What are we? Where are we going?* And in the upper right corner of the now famous painting he signed his name and dated it. Today this painting hangs in the Museum of Fine Arts in Boston, Massachusetts, USA.

William Wordsworth tells us in his poem "Intimations of Immortality" that we come from God, "who is our home." I experienced the poet's intuitive insight in my fourth past-life regression when I went back to the origin of my existence in the Body of God where all souls come from; but what made my regression so memorable was that I did not have reflective self-consciousness. I was an atom of God without an "I", and I was sent into the world to evolve through life for the divine purpose of creating a new "I" of God, which I also experienced in the same regression when I experienced the birth of my reflective self-consciousness in my first primordial human lifetime as the alpha male of a small group of higher primates, and I grew in my own identity as far as nature could take me through the natural process of karma and reincarnation and was called in my current lifetime to take evolution into my own hands to complete what nature could not finish, which I did when *the merciful law of divine synchronicity* introduced Gurdjieff into my life and I gave birth to my immortal self in my mother's kitchen one day; and that answers Paul Gauguin's famous three questions.

Where do we come from? We come from God. *What are we?* We are atoms of God, or sparks of divine consciousness as poets and mystics have intuited. *Where are we going?* We are going back home to God where we came from. We come from God as nascent souls with soul consciousness but no reflective self-consciousness, and we are destined to evolve through life and return to God as spiritually self-realized souls of God.

As incredible as it may seem, this has been my experience; but I cannot expect anyone to believe my story because like my hero Carl Gustav Jung, I am very familiar with what he called "the problem of resistance to understanding," which was Jung's insight into man's instinctive defense against whatever threatens one's sense of self.

I explored Jung's insight into man's "resistance to understanding" in a spiritual musing that I posted on my blog on *Saturday, March 19, 2016*. In this musing I wanted to explore the idea that when push comes to shove everything we believe is true in its own way, including my own strange story of self-discovery; so allow me to quote my spiritual musing before I offer an explanation for the rich young man's dilemma in Christ's parable: —

What If It's All True?

I wonder a lot. I always have. And the other day I wondered about why we all have a tendency to offer our opinion so freely, some of us more insistently than others.

"Why do you suppose that is?" I asked my life partner, Penny Lynn. We were out for a Sunday drive. We picked up a coffee at Tim Hortons in Elmvale and drove down to the Horseshoe Valley Road and on through the charming little village of Craighurst and then to Midland where we were going to pick up a pizza for dinner, and we tossed our points of view back and forth and saw that there were many reasons why we like to offer our opinion on practically everything; but essentially we felt it was because we like to think we are more right than others, and that's when I recalled something that St. Padre Pio said to me in one of my sessions with the psychic medium who channeled him for my novel *Healing with Padre Pio*: "**Resist the urge to be right.**"

"That was the best piece of advice that I got in my entire life," I said to Penny Lynn, because I had the annoying habit of always interrupting people because I felt that I was more right than they were, and I loved to quote different authors to back up my opinion, which only annoyed people further; but I wasn't conscious of this irritating habit until the Good Saint brought it to my attention, and then I saw just how exasperating I could be, which was why in that session, or another (I can't remember which) St. Padre Pio told me that I had a way of "chafing" people. *No wonder, given my annoying habit!*

"Ego's a big factor, then," I said to Penny Lynn. "Ego wants attention. That's why we love to offer our opinions so freely."

Donald Trump, the billionaire candidate for the leadership of the Republican Party for the upcoming American election, came to mind because of his brutish, massive ego; but I honestly can't fault Trump today for his massive ego, because I *know* now how important ego is for our growth and individuation. What Trump and all egoists don't know however, is that ego will one day have to be humbled for one to fulfill their destined purpose of wholeness and completeness which Jesus spoke to in one of his most misunderstood parables, the parable of the rich young man; but that's another musing for another day. Today I want to explore what I said to Penny on our Sunday drive: "It doesn't really matter, because it's all true."

Again, this falls into the category of spiritual musings that I call dangerous; not because this is what I have come to believe in my study of the human condition, which threatens the status quo, but because of what C. G. Jung referred to as "the problem of resistance to understanding."

Carl Gustav Jung, the pre-eminent Swiss psychologist who gave us a psychology of personality types and such words as *introvert, extrovert, synchronicity* (meaningful coincidence), *collective unconscious,* and *shadow* (the repressed side of our ego personality), was troubled by some of his patients (he saw up to eight patients a day for decades and analyzed more than eighty thousand dreams over his long career); he could not fathom why they had a resistance to understanding (which he later saw as an instinctive defense mechanism); and, I have to admit, this troubled me also until I learned the reason why in Jung's letter to Hans Schmid (*November 6, 1914*) in which he related how a vision that St. Brigitta of Sweden (1303-1373) had that clarified this problem of resistance to understanding that plagued his practice and his life.

In his letter, Jung wrote: "In a vision she saw the devil, who spoke to God, and had the following to say about the psychology of devils: 'Their belly is so swollen because their greed was boundless, for they filled themselves and were not sated, and so great was their greed that, had they been able to gain the whole world, they would gladly have exerted themselves, and would moreover have desired to reign in heaven...So the devil is a devourer. Understanding is likewise a devourer. Understanding swallows you up...Understanding is a fearfully binding power, at times a veritable murder of the soul as soon as it flattens out vital important differences. The core of the individual is a mystery of life, which is snuffed out when it is 'grasped'" (*Selected Letters of G. G. Jung, 1909-1961*, pp. 4-5).

The "psychology of devils" is the psychology of the ego, because ego has an insatiable appetite for life; that's why ego can never get enough of life. This is why we have a natural resistance to understanding, because understanding has a tendency to "flatten out vitally important differences and "snuff" out one's sense of self.

In short, one's ego does not want to be devoured by the devil (another ego), and we resist understanding because it preserves who we are. This is why Jung came to the conclusion that he did about the problem of resistance to understanding that hindered his patient's psychic healing, and his relationships with people.

"We should be connivers of our own mysteries, but veil our eyes chastely before the mystery of the other, so far as, being unable to understand himself, he does not need the 'understanding' of others," concluded Jung in his letter.

Ironically, ego is not our core identity, as Jesus knew only too well; which leads me to the dangerous theme of today's musing—the ontology of who we are and who we are not, the *being* and *non-being* of our nature: our inner and outer self...

Why would I say to Penny Lynn, "It doesn't really matter, because it's all true"? Did I mean that every person's opinion is true?

Yes, that's exactly what I meant. And this is the danger of today's spiritual musing, because it sounds like moral relativism which I deplore (see my spiritual musing "The Stupidity of Moral Relativism" in my book *The Armchair Guru*); but when personal opinion is seen in the context of our ontology (the *being* and *non-being* of our nature), it makes good sense why we might believe that we are more right than others.

It took many years to come to this realization, but our personal identity is made up of the individuated consciousness of the vital energy of life that has been called by many names— Divine Spirit, Chi, Tao, Baraka, and Logos to name a few; which means that our *being* is the consciousness of our essential nature (our inner self), and our *non-being* is the consciousness of our ego personality (our outer self) and which, as paradoxical as it may be, are both real because they are made of the same "stuff" of life. This is why I said to Penny Lynn that it doesn't really matter, because it's all true.

But this is an impossible concept to convey, and the only way I can possibly give it more clarity would be by saying that consciousness is one but has many levels depending upon its medium of expression, and when consciousness is expressed by way of our *non-being* (our ego/shadow personality) it is more opaque than when it is expressed by way of our *being* (our essential self); and at the risk of being annoying, let me quote something that Gurdjieff said that may put this musing into a less opaque perspective: "To speak the truth is the most difficult thing in the world; and one must study a great deal and for a long time in order to be able to speak the truth. The wish alone is not enough. *To speak the truth, one must know what the truth is and what a lie is, and first of all in oneself. And this nobody wants to know*" (*In Search of the Miraculous*, P. D. Ouspensky, p. 22). This is why man has a natural resistance to understanding: he refuses to see his own *non-being*...

THE MERCIFUL LAW OF DIVINE SYNCHRONICITY

As we pulled onto Highway 12 on our way to Pizza Pizza in Midland, I said to Penny Lynn, "You have no idea what a relief it is to know that whatever people say is true in its own way," which brought to mind something that I heard on *Judge John Deed* on TV the night before. Judge Deed asked an expert witness in the witness box (an elderly medical doctor who was an authority on the subject of inquiry) if she thought that the point in question was true, and she replied: "At my age, I have come to see that there are many variations of the truth." That's what I meant when I said, "It doesn't really matter, because it's all true." *But what a dangerous point of view!*

Donald Trump, the real estate mogul currently running for the American presidency, is a very rich man. A billionaire, he tells us. And he has a very big ego. Massive, in fact. He is brash, rash, crude, and entitled by wealth and power; but he is no less mortal than any other person in the world, because his wealth does not automatically grant him eternal life.

Ironically, we are all eternal because we are all born with an immortal soul; but for the sake of my story, given the paradigm of man's spiritual ignorance of his immortal nature, we can assume that man is not conscious of his immortal soul, and just like the rich young man in Christ's parable we would all love to have eternal life.

This parable has troubled man from the day Jesus gave it to the world, but could anyone possibly imagine Donald Trump giving away all of his riches to the poor in exchange for the consciousness of his immortal nature? Hardly, for such is the power of our *non-being*. And that's the tragedy of a literally interpretation of Christ's parable of the rich young man.

Jesus was speaking in the code of the secret way of Soul, and only one who has broken the code can appreciate the irony of Christ's parable—because the rich young man wasn't asked to give away his riches to the poor to gain eternal life; he was asked to give away his egoic attachment to his riches, which he could not do because he identified so strongly with his riches that if he gave them away he would no longer be himself. But which self would he cease to be if not the *non-being* of his ego personality?

Given this glimpse into the secret way of Soul, Jesus makes much more sense now when he said: ***"He that loveth his life shall lose it; and he that hateth his life in this world shall keep it unto life eternal."*** Which is precisely what I did when I lived my *Royal Dictum*, my "edict" of self-denial; and I "died" to my "false" self to "find" my true self.

I have explained the paradoxical nature of this process of conscious spiritual self-realization in my chapter "The Selfless Self" in my novel *Healing with Padre Pio,* and even more fully in *The Pearl of Great Price* which tells the story of how I found the most precious treasure in the world (my spiritual self), but suffice to say for now that until we learn the art of making our two selves into one will we ever realize the consciousness of our immortal nature; and this nobody wants to do until life makes them ready for the secret way. This is what Jesus meant when he said, ***"Many are called but few are chosen."***

The rich young man was called, but he was not chosen because he wasn't ready yet to "hear" what Jesus had to say…

9. PILGRIMAGE AND PENANCE

"There are no shortcuts to your true self..."

I was so excited when I broke the code of the secret way that I wrote a fantasy novel called *Jesus Wears Dockers, The Gospel Conspiracy Story* to give my reader a fictional account of how the process of conscious spiritual self-realization works in Christ's sayings and parables, but I was afraid to have it published because I felt it was too presumptuous, and I put it away in a plastic storage bin in the basement and forgot about it.

But when I "met" St. Padre Pio in my spiritual healing sessions with the psychic medium who channeled him for my novel *Healing with Padre Pio,* he told me that I was afraid to go back to my novel because I did not want to revisit my Christian faith that had caused me so much pain and suffering, and he encouraged me to take it out and get it published because it would help to heal my wounded Christian soul; and I did as he suggested.

After all, I had gone to St. Padre Pio to grind my Christian axes, and I poured all of my anger into my novel as I re-worked it, and I don't think I ever experienced creative writing at its most cathartic as I did when I brought *Jesus Wears Dockers* to resolution, because as I reworked my novel from the distance of its first writing I had the wisdom and objectivity to do it the creative justice it deserved, and my psychic medium even said that she thought that was the reason I had been called to have my spiritual healing with St. Padre Pio.

But as true as that may have been, writing my novel *Healing with Padre Pio* served many objectives, some of which I have yet to realize; but the most comforting thing it did for me was give me the strength to walk away from the New Age spiritual teaching of the Light and Sound of God that I had been living for the better part of thirty years but which kept me from unfolding in my destined purpose, and I posted a spiritual musing on my blog on *June 27, 2015* to express my newfound wisdom that I had realized writing *Healing with Padre Pio*, which I brought to resolution with my closing chapter

"The Vanity of All Spiritual Paths," a fitting description for that New Age teaching that I finally walked away from: —

Shadow Masters

"Man's shadow, I thought, is his vanity."
Friedrich Nietzsche

While working on my new book *The Man of God Walks Alone* (a literary exercise in what Carl Jung called "active imagination" in which I dialogue with my Oracle, St. Padre Pio), I was introduced to the concept of Shadow Masters by St. Padre Pio, who may or may not be an archetypal manifestation of my unconscious not unlike Jung's spiritual guide Philemon whom he later called his "superior insight," and so acutely conscious did I become of these false teachers from intimate personal experience that I was prompted by my Muse to explore this concept of Shadow Masters in today's spiritual musing, though admittedly under protest...

Heraclitus, the Greek philosopher who said that we cannot step into the same river twice, believed that life is always in a state of flux and is forever being transformed from one thing into another; and from this perspective was born Carl Jung's understanding of *enantiodromia*, the concept that everything will in time turn into its opposite, which gave birth to Jung's psychology of individuation whose ultimate purpose is to integrate the conflicting shadow side of our psychic self with our conscious ego personality, or what Jesus simply called "salvation."

The word salvation has a lot of baggage, but if one is fortunate enough to break the code of Christ's teaching and catch a glimpse of the secret way one will see that by salvation Jesus meant breaking the cycle of life and death by transcending the dual consciousness of our personality (our *being* and *non-*

being), which Jesus referred to as making the two into one as he tells us in one of his cryptic sayings: "For when the master himself was asked by someone when the kingdom would come, he said, **'When the two will be one, and the outer like the inner, and the male with the female neither male nor female'"** (*The Unknown Sayings of Jesus,* Marvin Meyer, p. 95).

This is the mystical nature of the individuation process that Carl Jung devoted his whole life to understanding and expounded upon in his magnum opus *Mysterium Coniunctionis* that he finally completed before dying, but try as he may he could not quite break the code of how to facilitate the mystical marriage of our inner and outer self and only brought us to the gateway of the kingdom of our true self; but the mystic philosopher/teacher Gurdjieff knew the secret way, and with his teaching of "work on oneself" I integrated my *being* and *non-being* and realized my transcendent self in my mother's kitchen one day as she kneaded bread dough on the kitchen table.

So I speak with the confidence of gnostic certainty about the secret way, and it behoves me now to shed some light upon this concept of Shadow Masters that pass themselves off as genuine Spiritual Masters, and so effectively I might add that they can ensnare the keenest seeker in the seductive web of their deception, as I have already illustrated in my spiritual musing "My Parable of the Packages." But why? What drives these people to deceive?

That's the mystery of Shadow Masters that I've been called upon to unravel; but so confounding is this mystery that I have no choice but to declare my ignorance, and I'm obliged to call upon my "superior insight" for assistance—

"What's my point of entry?"
"The becoming of man's nature."
"The being and non-being of our becoming?"
"One cannot exist without the other."
"All I know is that to be, we must become; and to become we have to transform the false into the real. That's the only way we

can make the two into one. So what's the purpose of a Shadow Master whose imperative is to keep soul trapped in one's non-being, or ego/shadow personality?"

"*Aye, there's the rub!*"

"You tease me."

"*If I may, wherein lies the proof of the pudding?*"

"In the experience."

"*Well?*"

"I loved the pudding at first, but the more I ate the less I liked it; and then the pudding gave me indigestion, and I had to walk away from the table. The first time with an offshoot Christian solar cult teaching that did irreparable damage to my eyesight, and then with a New Age teaching of the Light and Sound of God that gravely wounded my swollen pride when I learned that the modern day founder of this purloined ancient teaching was a fraudulent mythologizer."

"*One must eat the shadow to taste the shadow—*"

"STOP! I've got it! Shadow Masters serve shadow pudding!"

"*They too serve the Creator.*"

"What irony! Okay, I can take it from here..."

Shadow pudding? What on earth is that? That's the mystery, isn't it? But how else can we know the real unless we get our fill of the false?

And that's the Shadow Master's divine mission, to serve us shadow pudding until we get sick of it as I did with my spiritual path; but just what is this shadow pudding that tastes so good to the innocent seeker's palate?

For the better part of thirty years I feasted on the shadow pudding of this New Age spiritual teaching of the Light and Sound of God, but when I had my fill I began to get indigestion every time I dined at the Shadow Master's table; and then one night I had a dream that broke the spell of the Shadow Master's hold upon his followers, and I stopped eating and walked away from his table; hence my inspiration for today's spiritual musing.

In their exquisitely informative book *Meeting the Shadow, The Hidden Power of the Dark Side of Human Nature*, Editors Connie Zweig and Jeremiah Abrams wrote the following warning for all spiritual seekers: —

"However, for most participants in the new age, the shadow has been conspicuous by its absence. Seekers are often led to believe that, with the right teacher and the right practice, they can transcend to higher levels of awareness without dealing with their more petty vices or ugly emotional attachments. As Colorado journalist Marc Barasch puts it: 'Spirituality, as repackaged for the new age, is a confection of love and light, purified of pilgrimage and penance, of defeat and descent, of harrowing and humility'" (*Meeting the Shadow*, p. 130).

"Purified of pilgrimage and penance." That's the sweet ingredient of shadow pudding that appeals to the seeker's palate, just as Christianity's shadow pudding of instant salvation through Jesus without the purifying effort of pilgrimage and penance appeals to millions of Christians, which belies the law of spiritual growth through the pilgrimage and penance process of integrating our unconscious shadow with our conscious ego personality. Making the two into one, as Jesus said.

There are no shortcuts into the kingdom of one's true self, as Jesus tells us in his parable of the pearl of great price, and shadow pudding feeds the shadow and starves the soul with vacuous truisms like *"You are Soul"* and *"Soul exists because God loves you"* that serve only to eliminate the pilgrimage and penance process of our *becoming*.

Without the purifying pilgrimage and penance process of our *becoming*, we will never make the two into one and become conscious of our spiritual nature; but Shadow Masters are relentless, and they will do whatever it takes to keep followers dining at their sumptuous table of deceptions, like using fear to ensure absolute obedience.

"What makes me sick at heart? When people I know and love decide to leave. That will delay their entry into the highest states of consciousness," wrote the Shadow Master of my spiritual path in his quarterly *Letter to High Initiates*, threatening those who think of leaving his teaching of the Light and Sound of God that I finally walked away from after dining at his table for more than thirty years; and though I have a sour taste in my mouth from all the shadow pudding that I ate, especially the fear that he implanted in my mind with sugar-coated kindness that salvation was not possible without his inner and outer guidance, I still want to thank him for his teaching which took me through a fabled country of duplicity and brought me back home to reality, because now I *know* that Shadow Masters are only as real as we allow them to be. As St. Padre Pio said to me, *"Life is a journey of growth and understanding,"* and I had grown enough to see that I was ready to be my own master, as every soul must be to complete their destined purpose to wholeness and completeness.

―――

What spared me the humiliation of total self-deception, which most followers of this New Age teaching of the Light and Sound of God are afflicted with, was the birth of my immortal self that I experienced before taking up this spiritual path, because from the perspective of my transcendent self I *knew* that the Inner Master that the Spiritual Leader of this New Age teaching purported to be was my own "superior insight," and not him; so I was free of the greatest deception of this teaching that he was our Inner and Outer Master.

But alas, I was not as free as I thought I was or it would not have taken so long to break free of this Shadow Master's hold upon me, and I can only attribute this to my own spiritual conceit (after all, I did look into the Face of God, which I may reveal in my story if I dare to risk it); which was why *the merciful law of divine synchronicity* called me to the gifted medium who inspired my novel *Healing with Padre Pio*, because with each spiritual healing session that I had I became more humbled by St. Padre Pio, and his unbearable compassion finally slew the proud demon of my spiritual conceit.

But why did *the merciful law of divine synchronicity* call me to the psychic medium whose spiritual guide St. Padre Pio helped resolve my anger at Christianity?

That's the mystery of *the intelligent guiding principle of life,* and if my understanding of the secret way holds any merit it's because my spiritual path of the New Age teaching of the Light and Sound of God had brought me to an insurmountable impasse of illusion and self-deception and I needed providential guidance to break free of the unconscious hold it had upon me, which I got with my inspiration to write my novel *Healing with Padre Pio*; that's how I came to *see* the merciful nature of the divine agency of synchronicity...

10. A BREATHTAKING KIND OF NIHILISM

"Synchronicity is an act of grace...."

I've always had one foot in writing, but when I walked away from the New Age spiritual path of the Light and Sound of God that I had lived for the better part of thirty years, I stepped into writing with both feet and learned to trust my creative unconscious implicitly, as every writer must, which I put to the test with my new memoir *The Summoning of Noman* that was inspired by a strong "nudge" to go online and do some research on C. G. Jung who had a great influence upon my life, which **serendipitously** led me to the documentary *The Way of the Dream* by Jungian analyst Marion Woodman and her Jungian analyst brother Frazer Boa, which in turn "inspired" me to keep a new dream journal to study my dreams, because dreams being the language of the soul as Jung believed I wanted to see what my unconscious was trying to tell me; thus my new book *The Summoning of Noman,* a study of my journey to my true self through the message of my dreams.

A writer has to have his own voice to speak his truth, otherwise he's always in danger of mouthing the truth of others; but not all writers find their own voice, and they write and write and write hoping to find it one day. That's what happened to me. And by the time I brought *The Summoning of Noman* to closure with the dream that inspired my closing chapter ("Canned Opinions, Personal Beliefs, Prejudices, and My Own Voice") my unconscious confirmed that I had finally found my own voice, and a great relief came over me.

So, just what does it mean for a writer to find his own voice? What is this great literary mystery that writers do not understand but know if they have a voice or not? And is it the same voice for all writers—poets, novelists, playwrights, and essayists? Is it an individual voice that speaks to universal truths of the human condition, or is it a collective voice that speaks to the individual truths of the human condition? Is it both? **What is a writer's voice?**

THE MERCIFUL LAW OF DIVINE SYNCHRONICITY

It took ten years of writing before it finally dawned upon me that my desire for writing was far greater than my talent, and another ten years of writing before I cultivated any talent worth exploring; but I could not help myself, I *had* to write.

But finding my true self was my first priority, and I spent my best energies reading and seeking and making a living; and I had to satisfy my desire for writing within the context of my first priority of seeking my true self, and also making a living. Which is why I carried a notebook with me everywhere I went in my contract painting business, and like James Joyce I jotted down many "epiphanies."

By epiphany Joyce meant a showing forth, something more than an impression; on the contrary, for the author of *A Portrait of the Artist as a Young Man* (which I read in high school), epiphanies guide a deeper insight into the truth of things. But what is the truth of things that epiphanies show forth? What do epiphanies reveal, or point to?

Adrienne Rich would say that epiphanies reveal or point to the "what is" of the human condition. Her definition of poetry is *"an act of the imagination that transforms reality into a deeper perception of what is,"* and what is this "what is" if not the essential truth and meaning of the human condition? But few writers penetrate this secret, and those that do are very circumspect in how they reveal it—like the poet Emily Dickinson.

On *Saturday, March 5, 2016* I posted a spiritual musing on my blog in which I disclose the mystery of what Adrienne Rich calls the "what is" of the human condition that I joyfully discovered in Emily Dickinson's poetry, and for the sake of this story, I will quote my spiritual musing and then explore the mystery of "what is" further: —

The Mystique of Emily Dickinson's Poetry

"This life is the way, the long sought-after way to the unfathomable, which we call divine. There are no other ways, all other ways are false paths."

THE RED BOOK
C. G. Jung

Although I came to Emily Dickinson's poetry late in life, despite having a copy of *Emily Dickinson Selected Poems* on my shelf all these many years, it wasn't until I was nudged to read her poetry for a book that I was writing did my heart leap with joy when I discovered that Emily Dickinson was an intuitive *knower* of the secret way that she concealed in her poetry; and I went online and watched and listened to all the You Tube videos and podcasts on Emily Dickinson and her poetry that I could find.

I watched and listened to Dickinson readers and scholars and Professors of Literature and biographers of her life and I couldn't get over how she perplexed them all to a person, including the pre-eminent literary critic Professor Harold Bloom who said, "She baffles us by the power of her mind." But what they all failed to grasp, and with good reason, which Dickinson hints at in her poetry (sometimes playfully, sometimes ruthlessly, but always to protect herself), was the secret way of life that she had made her mindful path to her true self.

"My business is circumference," wrote Dickinson in a letter, and by "circumference" she meant the fullness and completeness of her life, or what Jesus referred to as making the two into one: "For when the master himself was asked by someone when his kingdom would come, he said: **'When the two will be one, and the outer like the inner, and the male with the female neither male nor female'**" (*The Unknown Sayings of Jesus*, Marvin Meyer).

But this is heady stuff, and not many people want to go there for fear of how the world will react to the moral imperative of the secret way; which is why Dickinson wrote Poem 1263—*and with characteristic irony, I might add!* —that one has to be as wise as a serpent and as gentle as a dove to reveal the sacred truth of the secret way of life: —

> Tell all the truth but tell it slant –
> Success in Circuit lies
> Too bright for our infirm Delight

THE MERCIFUL LAW OF DIVINE SYNCHRONICITY

> The Truth's superb Surprise
> As Lightening to the Children eased
> With explanation kind
> The Truth must dazzle gradually
> Or every man be blind –

"Poetry is an act of the imagination that transforms reality into a deeper perception of what is," said Adrienne Rich, a lover of Dickinson's poetry; and focussing on the mundane reality of her reclusive life, Emily Dickinson transformed the simple moments of her daily routine into such a deep perception of the truth of her life that she tapped into the truth of her soul's purpose— "Adventure most unto itself /The Soul condemned to be; /Attended by a Single Hound – /Its own Identity."

This is the attraction of Emily Dickinson's poetry—the pursuit of her own Identity, like Francis Thompson's *Hound of Heaven*. Her poetry is her "letter to the world," a map of her path to her true self, which makes it endlessly fascinating because every path to one's true self speaks the sacred truth of the secret way through one's own voice, if one but have the eyes to see and ears to hear. This is why so many lovers of poetry get hooked on Emily Dickinson: *her poetry speaks to one's soul.*

How she did it, no one knows (perhaps she revealed it in her letters, which I have not read yet; or maybe in one of her poems which I will look for when I get her collected works), but Dickinson awakened to the secret way and made it her life's goal to realize her soul's purpose. As she said, "My business is circumference," making this the axis of her life which superseded all of her other interests; but why the imperative? Why the urgency? Why the drama? That's what I'm exploring in today's spiritual musing...

The curious thing about writing my spiritual musings is that they don't always go where I expect them to, and although I was called to write today's musing by an idea set free by one of Emily's poems, my musings have a mind of their own.

For years I've been toying with writing a spiritual musing on the "props" that people depend upon to support their self-image—stylish clothes, nice home, winter vacations, a never-ending supply of status symbols; but the "props" that I was called to focus on for today's spiritual musing were those "props" that Dickinson symbolized in one of her most esoteric poems on the moral imperative of the secret way—Poem 729:

> The Props assist the House
> Until the House is built
> And then the Props withdraw
> And adequate, erect,
> The House support itself
> And cease to recollect
> The Auger and the Carpenter –
> Just such a retrospect
> Hath the perfected Life –
> A past of Plank and Nail
> And slowness – then the Scaffolds drop
> Affirming it a Soul –

"House" is Emily Dickinson's symbol for what Jesus called building one's house upon a rock and psychologist C. G. Jung called "wholeness and singleness of self," and "building" one's "House" takes what Gurdjieff called *"conscious effort"* and *"intentional suffering,"* but making the inner and the outer into one self with no hypocrisy demands all the moral integrity that one can muster; and when one has completed what nature cannot finish and perfected one's life, one can throw away the props because they have affirmed their soul's purpose. But this can take a lifetime, if one is ready.

"Many are called but few are chosen," said Jesus, addressing the hard reality of one's evolution through life; and only when life has made one ready for the secret way will one hear their soul's cry for "wholeness and singleness of self," which

THE MERCIFUL LAW OF DIVINE SYNCHRONICITY

Emily Dickinson did and shared in her "letter to the world." But her "letter" can be puzzling.

"Dickinson waits for us perpetually up the road from our tardiness," said Professor Harold Bloom, humbly confessing that to catch up to Emily Dickinson one has to *know* how to get there, which few people do; but the irony of her poetry is that the secret way cannot be seen by those that do not live it. *And that's the mystique of Emily Dickinson's poetry.*

I've only read one of his novels (*The Women*) and some of his short stories in *The New Yorker*, but T. C. Boyle is a very talented writer with his own distinct voice who admits to losing his Christian faith at the tender age of sixteen, and after years of searching for the "what is" of the human condition he went on to embrace the nihilistic philosophy of existentialism. "I wish I had better news," he said in an interview online, "but I just can't find it."

This is the tragedy of many writers, including the greatest writer of the western world, if not the whole world, William Shakespeare whom Professor Harold Bloom calls the god of literature—perhaps an allusion to James's Joyce's comment about writers being like God who create their own world; but for all of his genius, Bloom's god of literature is tragic.

"Ultimately the elliptical burden of what Shakespeare gives us is a breathtaking kind of nihilism more uncanny than anything that Nietzsche apprehended," said Professor Bloom with a sadness of heart and heaviness of soul in an interview that I caught online. *"I think in the end he, among so much, is telling us that there are no values or value except those we create or imbue events, people, and things with. Emerson beautifully said, 'No world, there is no next world. Here and now is the whole fact...the rest is silence,"* Bloom added, which brought me to tears because the great literary scholar's sadness overwhelmed me. It was as though he was saying, "If Shakespeare couldn't find a way out, no one can."

That's what the existentialist Jean Paul Sartre concluded. Man is condemned by his own freedom and must posit his own values to make life worth living; but the terror of moral relativism is that man may be wrong in the values that he posits to give his life meaning and purpose, as Albert Camus realized with his novel *The Fall,* and the tragic consequence of the unresolved writer's perspective on the human condition is, as Professor Bloom concluded, nothing more than "a breathtaking kind of nihilism."

But I could never imagine Sisyphus happy, and unlike T. C. Boyle who echoes Sartre and Camus and quite possibly Bloom's supreme god of literature (I'm not quite convinced that Bloom is right about Shakespeare's nihilism, however breathtaking), I have better news; but I am not alone in my discovery of the "what is" of the human condition.

I have no doubt that Shakespeare knew the human heart better than any other writer, and that his epiphanies of the human soul speak to the universal truth of man's absurd limitations; but not until a writer has intuited the art of making the two into one will they resolve the paradox of man's *being* and *non-being* and transcend the *enantiodromiac* nature of the human condition, which Emily Dickinson points to in her poetry:

> So I must baffle at the Hint
> And cipher at the Sign
> And make much blunder, if at last
> I take the clue divine —

"I am out with lanterns looking for myself," wrote Dickinson, and she got another "Hint" one day, perhaps staring out the window, dusting her book shelf, or while sipping a fresh cup of tea while working on another poem, a "clue divine," but what is her "clue divine" if not an epiphany, a showing forth of the "what is" of the human condition that she carefully concealed in her poetry as soul's essential purpose of affirming its own "Identity"?

As John Keats realized with poetic genius, soul comes into the world to create its own identity, "a bliss peculiar to each one by individual existence," which is why I concluded in my own search for my true self that **our greatest need in life is to be ourselves**; but, as I learned only too sadly in my unrelenting journey of self-discovery, to be ourselves we have to *become* ourselves by mastering the art of making our inner and outer self into one self with no hypocrisy, what Emily Dickinson called the "circumference" of her life, and that's the "what is" of my life experience that speaks the voice of the secret way that Jesus concealed in his cryptic saying of building one's house upon a rock: —

"Therefore whosoever heareth these sayings of mine, and doeth them, I will liken him unto a wise man, which built his house upon a rock. And the rain descended, and the floods came, and the winds blew, and beat upon that house; and it fell not, for it was built upon a rock. And everyone that heareth these sayings of mine, and doeth them not, shall be likened unto a foolish man, which built his house upon sand. And the rain descended, and the floods came, and the winds blew, and beat upon that house; and it fell: and great was the fall of it" (Matthew 7: 24-27).

Jesus is talking about the secret way in this saying. If one lives the secret way according to his teachings (***"whosever doeth these sayings of mine"),*** he will grow in the consciousness of his eternal self ***("built his house upon a rock");*** and if one does not live the secret way according to his sayings, he will grow in the consciousness of his egoic self (***"built his house upon sand"***) which will be subject to inevitable karmic dissolution.

This is the impenetrable mystery that Emily Dickinson caught a glimpse of, which her biographer Richard Sewell (*The Life of Emily Dickinson*) discerned from her cryptic poetry and letters. "What she tells us is, again and again, what it feels like to be alive," said Richard Sewell in *Voices and Visions: Emily Dickinson (1988)*. "And that is her gift, a steady march and a pilgrimage, I would say, towards some kind of unity, some kind of belief, something that would bring the whole thing together. She called it, in the word she was fond of using, circumference. 'My business,' she said in a letter, 'is circumference.'"

By the miracle of her poetic genius, Emily Dickinson broke the code and saw *the omniscient guiding principle of life* as it spoke to her throughout the day, which to me was not a mystery because this is how I became conscious of the secret way as I "worked" on myself with Gurdjieff's teaching, my *Royal Dictum,* and the sayings of Jesus; but Dickinson was not the only poet who broke the secret code of *the omniscient guiding principle of life.* So did William Wordsworth, whose poem "Character of the Happy Warrior" reveals the identity of the Happy Warrior as the "generous Spirit" of the secret way of life:

> Who is the Happy Warrior? Who is he
> That every man in arms should wish to be?
> –It is the generous Spirit, who, when brought
> Among the tasks of real life, hath wrought
> Upon the plan that pleased his boyish thought:
> Whose high endeavors are an inward light
> That makes the path before him always bright…

The Happy Warrior "labors good on good to fix, and owes /To virtue every triumph that he knows," which makes "virtue" the key that unlocks the mystery of the secret way; and the more "virtue" one acquires, the more they will be blessed by *the omniscient guiding principle of the secret way,* as Wordsworth was one day when he fell into despair.

"We poets begin in gladness, /But thereof come in the end despondency and madness," wrote Wordsworth in his poem "Resolution and Independence." After a night of wind and rain, the sun rose and the all the birds were singing and Wordsworth went for a walk on the lonely moor to enjoy the freshness of a new day; but out of nowhere his demon spirit of melancholy floods his mind—"As high as we have mounted in delight /In our dejection do we sink as low; / To me that morning did it happen so; /And fears and fancies thick upon me came; / Dim sadness—blind thoughts, I knew not, nor could name."

So there's the poet walking in the fresh morning air after a night of wind and rain enjoying the birds singing and a hare plashing about with joy when thoughts of sadness and melancholy possess him and pull him down into despair, and he continues walking drowning in dejection; but then **serendipity** happens— "whether it were by peculiar grace, /A leading from above, a something given"—he chances upon a Man, "the oldest man he seemed that wore grey hairs," conning a pond for leeches, and the melancholy poet takes a stranger's privilege and strikes a conversation with the old traveler:

THE MERCIFUL LAW OF DIVINE SYNCHRONICITY

> "The old Man still stood talking by my side;
> But now his voice to me was like a stream
> Scarce heard; nor word from word could I divide;
> And the whole body of the Man did seem
> Like one whom I had met in a dream;
> Or like a man from some far region sent,
> To give me human strength, by apt admonishment.

What were the chances of Wordsworth coming upon the Leech Gatherer on the lonely moor as his mind became flooded with sadness and despair? The old Man's indomitable spirit drove out the lonely poet's demon of melancholy, and Wordsworth ends his poem with words that I have committed to memory to inspire me in my own moments of dejection: —

> I could have laughed myself to scorn to find
> In that decrepit Man so firm a mind.
> "God," said I, "be my help and stay secure;
> I'll think of the Leech Gatherer on the lonely moor!"

Given my many experiences with *the merciful law of divine synchronicity*, plus the hundreds of stories that I have read on this miraculous phenomenon, it wasn't a quantum leap for me to conclude that there is an *omniscient guiding principle of life* that choreographs our journey to wholeness and completeness, and it does so mercifully; and it wasn't a quantum leap for me to conclude that this *omniscient guiding principle of life* is the generous Spirit of the secret way and "what is" of the human condition that every writer seeks; and it wasn't a quantum leap for me to conclude that when a writer taps into *the omniscience guiding principle of the secret way* with the creative power of their gift, the universal truth of the human condition reveals itself through the prism of the writer's individuality; this is how a writer finds their own voice, because this is how I found mine. ***In short, a writer's voice is his individual view on the truth of the***

human condition, and no one else's; and a writer's individual view is the "what is" of the human condition as he experiences it.

11. THE PLAYFUL SPIRIT OF SYNCHRONICITY

"Life is not an old whore that screws us of our virtue..."

If, as I have come to see in my own journey of self-discovery, we are all sparks of divine consciousness destined to evolve through life to give birth to a new "I" of God through the natural evolutionary process of karma and reincarnation, which can only evolve us so far and no further, and if, as I have also come to see, we have to take evolution into our own hands to fulfill our destined purpose of realizing wholeness and singleness of self—making our two selves into one, as Jesus would say—it would not be a stretch for me to say that today's emerging philosophy of one Self is only half right.

I have neither the desire nor inclination to explore this age-old Buddhist concept of one Self, which for my own peace of mind I have already done in my third volume of spiritual musings *Stupidity Is Not a Gift of God* with my essay "On the Evolutionary Impulse to Individuate: A Response to the Spiritual Path of Evolutionary Enlightenment," but I do feel obliged to explain what I mean when I say that this ancient philosophy of one Self that is becoming popular today is only half right just as Sartre was only half right when he said, "I am what I am not, and I am not what I am." One's true Self is both one's *being* and *non-being* but neither; and that's the mystery that literature can only hint at, as Emily Dickinson does in her poetry when she speaks about the "circumference" of her life.

"Man is condemned to be free," concluded Sartre, the existentialist who was unable to resolve the paradoxical nature of man's *being* and *non-being*, condemned to freely posit his own values to give his life some sense of meaning and purpose, however fatuous it would be in light of his nihilistic philosophy. Which was why I came to tears when I heard the brilliant Yale scholar of Literature Professor Harold Bloom say, almost as though confessing to himself at what his life-long study of literature had brought him to, that his god of literature could not resolve the paradox of the human condition either, thus sadly rendering the noble bard's inimitable body of work into "a breathtaking kind of nihilism."

But it's not literary genius, or genius of any kind—be it artistic or scientific—that can square the circle of life and resolve the paradox of the human condition; it requires something more, which was what Katherine Mansfield concluded when she said to her friend and mentor A. R. Orage: "Suppose that I could succeed in writing as well as Shakespeare. It would be lovely, but what then? There is something wanting in literary art even at its highest. Literature is not enough." But enough for what, if not to realize wholeness and singleness of self that Katherine Mansfield desperately longed for. This is why she went to Gurdjieff.

"In the deepest sense I've always been disunited," she wrote to her husband, the writer John Middleton Murray from Gurdjieff's Institute in Fontainebleau where she went in the hope that Gurdjieff's teaching would be what she was looking for.

Katherine Mansfield had a longing in her soul that her selfish bohemian life could not satisfy, nor could her passion for literature, and she went to Gurdjieff because she heard he had a teaching that would satisfy her desperate longing to be whole; and although she never achieved her lofty goal, Orage tells us that she died "radiant in her new attitude."

But she was not the only writer to suffer from this tragic affliction of the soul, she gave it expression because she was a gifted writer; and though he was not as acutely conscious of his own affliction as Katherine Mansfield, the Nobel Laureate Saul Bellow had a terrifying moment of self-awareness on his deathbed which I explored in a spiritual musing that addresses this issue nicely. I've quoted this musing already in my twin soul book *Death, the Final Frontier*, but it bears repeating:

Was I a Man or a Jerk?
A Dying Writer's Last Question

THE MERCIFUL LAW OF DIVINE SYNCHRONICITY

I was online researching the Canadian-born American writer Saul Bellow, who won the Nobel Prize in Literature in 1976, and I came upon his son Greg Bellow talking about his memoir *Saul Bellow's Heart* that he wrote to show his father as he knew him growing up to balance out the impression of the lionized writer that the public had of his famous father, and Greg related a fascinating anecdote about his father's dying question that peaked my interest enough to explore the moral implications of that question in today's spiritual musing.

Even to the very end, Saul Bellow was in moral conflict with himself; why else would he ask his friend for an honest answer to the question "**was I a man or a jerk?**" Although I have only read two of Saul Bellow's books, his novella *The Actual* and *It All Adds Up*, a nonfiction collection of some of his work which includes his Nobel Lecture, and one short story called "The Silver Plate," I never read any of his major novels like *Humbold's Gift*, *Herzog*, and *Mr. Sammler's Planet* (the one I want to read is *Ravelstein*, which was based on his friend and author of *The Closing of the American Mind*, Professor Alan Bloom), but after all of my research on Bellow and his novels and listening to Zachary Leader talk about his biography *The Life of Saul Bellow* I elicited a strong impression of the writer that gave me a context to the final question of his long-lived life: "**was I a man or a jerk?**"

Why would a man who spent his whole life exploring the human condition in his novels ask such a question if he did not have moral reservations about his life? But let me relate the anecdote first as his son Greg told it in the You Tube video JST Presents: "Saul Bellow's Spiritual Quest," and then I can explore his father's disturbing death-bed question.

A man in the audience asked Saul's son Greg Bellow the question, "I wonder if you know the manner of his dying? Were you with him when he died?"

"I was not," Greg replied; and then the man asked, "Did you hear about how he handled the occasion?" That's when Greg related the anecdote of his father's final question.

Saul Bellow was in his bed at home dying and tended to by his fifth wife Janice, who was forty years his junior, and he was in and out of consciousness and had not awakened in a couple of days when his friend Gene Goodheart came to visit him.

"Saul, Saul," said his friend, trying to wake him up, and Saul opened his eyes and saw his friend and said, "Gene, I want to ask you a question if you give me an honest answer."

"You know I'll give you an honest answer," said Gene Goodheart.

And Saul said, "Gene, was I a man or a jerk?"

We don't know what Gene Goodheart answered, but Saul's son Greg interpreted his father's question to mean that he was still wrestling with his conscience. "In other words, he had moral courage to the end, to be able to assess himself, to be able to criticize himself. That's what I know, and I don't think he lasted another few days," he replied to the man who asked Greg about his father's death; but if I were asked to give an answer to Saul Bellow's dying question, I would have to say: he was both.

Saul Bellow was the same as any other person in the world, only more exaggerated because he was a very gifted writer who explored his own conflicted nature through his novels; that's why he was awarded the Nobel Prize in Literature *"for the human understanding and subtle analysis of contemporary culture that are combined in his work."* Like every writer who taps into the consciousness of their times and becomes a witness to their generation, Saul Bellow reflected the human condition in his fiction as he experienced it in the inescapable dynamic of his Jewish heritage, mostly focused on Chicago where he lived, just as every writer explores the same human condition in the dynamic of their own heritage, like mine for example which is Italian Canadian; but why would I say that this Quebec-born American Jewish writer who sacrificed everyone for his art was both a man and a jerk? That's what I hope to explore in today's spiritual musing...

"One cannot tell writers what to do. The imagination must find its own path," wrote Saul Bellow in his Nobel Lecture; but the path that the writer takes may take him closer to the truth of the human condition than most people can bear. That's why Bellow added, "Perhaps humankind cannot bear too much reality, but neither can it bear too much unreality, too much abuse of the truth" (*It All Adds Up*, "The Nobel Lecture," p. 95); and that's the dilemma that every writer must suffer, because the closer they get to the truth of the human condition the harder it is to bear it, which was why Saul Bellow's conscience forced him on his deathbed to ask his friend Gene Goodheart **"was I a man or a jerk?"**

Just as an aside, if I may be allowed a moment of personal humor, I find the fact that Saul Bellow should ask a friend named Gene Goodheart for an honest answer to his deathbed question **"was I a man or a jerk?"** to be so laden with irony that it would take a whole book to explain it; but it's enough to know that the spirit of synchronicity has a playful sense of humor, and why it has often been called the Trickster.

Being a writer, I am acutely conscious of the fact that we cannot escape what we are, which has been the inspiration for such great works of literature as *The Strange Case of Dr. Jekyll and Mr. Hyde* by Robert Louis Stevenson, and *The Picture of Dorian Grey* by Oscar Wilde; and Saul Bellow could not escape the fact that he was as much of a jerk (perhaps more so, depending upon one's relationship with him) as he was the man he tried to be, or wanted the world to believe he was.

But that's the dilemma that art cannot resolve, which was why the gifted young writer Katherine Mansfield told her redoubtable editor A. R. Orage that art was not enough and why I wrote in my own memoir *The Pearl of Great Price*, **"Stories bear the truth of the human condition, and the human condition is the story of our becoming; but not until we solve the riddle of our becoming will literature resolve the issue of the human condition."**

Saul Bellow could not resolve the issue of his personal condition with the creative genius of his fiction, which is why he spent years studying the spiritual teachings of Rudolph Steiner, the founding father of Anthroposophy, and why Katherine Mansfield sought out the mystic teacher Gurdjieff at his Institute for the Harmonious Development of Man in Fontainebleau, France to study his radical teaching of self-transformation just before she died of tuberculosis.

But what is the central issue of the human condition that art cannot resolve? That's the question that writers feel with every fiber of their being but cannot resolve with their art but which they have to explore to give expression to that *lump of painful truth pushing at their heart,* as another Nobel laureate Alice Munro expressed the writer's compulsion to write; what is this lump of painful truth that has to find expression in a writer's work?

The pre-eminent literary critic Professor Harold Bloom, author of *Novelists and Novels,* among many other brilliant books of literary criticism, caught a glimpse of this lump of painful truth pushing at Saul Bellow's heart and had this to say about the aesthetic mystery of Bellow's literary achievement: "His heroes are superb observers, worthy of their Whitmanian heritage. What they lack is Whitman's Real Me or Me Myself, or else they are blocked from expressing it" (*Novelists and Novels,* p. 419).

This "Real Me or Me Myself" is that lump of painful truth forever pushing at the writer's heart and what they seek with their fiction, which became the theme of my book *The Lion that Swallowed Hemingway,* because like Saul Bellow my literary mentor and high school hero Ernest Hemingway also died unresolved, which he confessed to in his memoir *A Moveable Feast,* the book that he was working on just before taking his own life with his favorite shotgun in Ketchum, Idaho.

"When I saw my wife again standing by the tracks as the train came in by the piled logs at the station, I wish I had died before I ever loved anyone but her," wrote Hemingway at the end of *A*

THE MERCIFUL LAW OF DIVINE SYNCHRONICITY

Moveable Feast, speaking of his first wife Hadley Richardson whom he betrayed with his affair with Pauline Pfeiffer, the woman who seduced and stole him away from Hadley but who was to be replaced by the journalist Martha Gellhorn, and she by his fourth wife Mary Welsh; and Saul Bellow's son Greg tells us in his memoir *Saul Bellow's Heart* that his father confessed to him that he wished he had never divorced Greg's mother, his first wife; but he did divorce her, and four more wives later he's in bed dying full of remorse and regrets.

And if I may, risking the esoteric flavor of my humor, I honestly feel that Saul Bellow's friend Gene Goodheart was providentially sent to visit Saul on his deathbed to let him know, in that synchronistic trickster way, that **lacking in the virtues of a good heart one will always risk being a jerk in life**. It was like the medieval morality play *The Summoning of Everyman* and **Mr. Good Heart** went to Saul, who was also summoned by God for a reckoning, and found him lacking in the virtues of a good heart, and the delicious irony of Saul Bellow's life was that he failed to see his answer to his dying question in his good friend Gene Goodheart's name!

I'd love to say that "Old Whore Life" was having a final cackle at Saul Bellow's famous literary life, but since I wrote *Old Whore Life, Exploring the Shadow Side of Karma* I know it wasn't the "Old Whore" laughing at the great author; it was merely Saul Bellow catching an honest guilt-ridden glimpse of his selfish life as he faced his final hour, and his death-bed question would be the equivalent of Camus's *"une prise de conscience"* that the philosopher of the absurd explored in his penitent novel *The Fall*, because there was an ironic absurdity to Saul Bellow's final question **"was I a man or a jerk?"**

Playing upon Flaubert's famous line *"Madame Bovary, c'est moi,"* I came to the same startling realization as I explored the shadow side of karma in my book *Old Whore Life* when it dawned upon me that the "Old Whore" was merely the shadow side of our own unresolved karma; and with bitter-sweet irony I shouted at the heavens— *"Old Whore Life, c'est moi!"*

It must have been the final straw when I wrote in one of my pocket notebooks that I carried around with me to catch all those Joycean epiphanies that came to me out of the blue each day, but I had to point my finger somewhere: **"Life is like an old whore that squats obscenely upon my shoulders and screws me of my virtue every chance she gets!"**

Something happened to me that day, another cruel blow from life that devastated me, and I had to blame someone for my misfortune; that's when I likened life to an old whore that loves to screw us of our virtue every chance she gets, and it took years of Gurdjieffian effort to transform my karmic self enough for me to see that I was the author of my own misery; and that's when I shouted at the heavens, *"Old Whore Life, c'est moi!"*

It's a long, long journey to this point of self-realization, which the eighty-nine year old Saul Bellow's death-bed question can attest to; but the great author was fortunate to even catch a glimpse of his shadow self a day or so before passing, because the unresolved shadow side of our personality is so finely blended with our ego that most people will go to their grave blind to their karmic nature; but not until we become aware of our own shadow and transform it with what Gurdjieff called *conscious effort* and *intentional suffering* and Socrates called "gathering and collecting soul into herself" will we satisfy the longing in our soul for wholeness and completeness, which takes my story to the question of **conscious evolution**…

12. THE MERCIFUL MYSTERY OF HUMAN SUFFERING

"I bring you the beauty of suffering..."

I remember years ago listening to an interview on CBC radio with the cartoonist-turned-evangelist-turned-agnostic Charles Templeton, whose autobiography *Farewell to God* tells the story of why in good conscience he had to reject his Christian faith, and he said something that stuck in my mind like crazy glue: **"Life is a hierarchy of devouring."**

Templeton couldn't fathom how an omnipotent loving God could be responsible for so much suffering in the world, and he abandoned his Christian faith and embraced Darwinian evolution and became an agnostic who summed up his life's wisdom in the following words: "I believe that, in common with all living creatures, we die and cease to exist as an entity."

"Wow!" I said to myself, incredulous of his soul-crushing nihilism. *"But that's what happens when one tries to pour the ocean into a tea cup,"* I added, with an ironic snicker; because that was the fundamental reason I dropped out of university where I had gone to study philosophy in my effort to find an answer to my question **"who am I?"**

I was born a "hound of heaven," and I had to go where the scent took me to find my true self; but good God, was it hard to break away when I had come to the end of another path, and when I decided to drop out of university I paid with desolation and heartbreak.

But I had no choice, I had vowed to find my true or die trying; which was why it was so unbearably painful to break up with the young lady that I began dating when I was called to drop my *Royal Dictum* and move on from my path of self-denial that I had taken up after I dropped out of university. Debbie and I dated for several years when one evening as we lay in front of the cozy fire in my separate apartment of my parents' home something inside me "snapped" and I saw Debbie for herself and not the woman I had fallen in love with in my mind, and I knew in that moment of startled awareness that I had to stop seeing her.

It wasn't fair to her, because I didn't love her for who she was; I was in love with an image in my mind that I had created of her. But when something "snapped" that evening as we lay in front of the fire (we were talking about books and Greek mythology), I saw Debbie for who she was and not what I imagined her to be; and the reality of her life was too much and shattered the illusory image of my beautiful lover, and I had to end our relationship.

But it cost me dearly, because she didn't deserve what I did to her. She was who she was, and I just didn't want to see *her*; and letting go of her was a very painful chapter in my journey of self-discovery, and we both suffered immeasurably. But I still had more suffering to do, because it happened again with another woman.

Several years later I dated Mary, who was older by twelve years, separated from her alcoholic husband, and with two children, one still in high school and the other married with one child, and we dated for seven months before I realized that our relationship would never be able to contain me, and I knew that if we continued I would suffer the unbearable anguish of feeling smothered by our relationship, and I had to end it. But I had learned from my breakup with Debbie to make it as painless as possible, and I wrote Mary a long letter explaining why we had to stop seeing each other, which I delivered to her in person.

She went into her living room to read the letter while I sat in the kitchen waiting, and when she finally came out, her eyes and nose red from crying, we hugged long and hard and I thanked her for being so understanding, and we parted company. But in all honesty, had not *the merciful law of divine synchronicity* prepared Mary for our breakup, she would have suffered much more than she did; and I thank divine providence for the intercession.

I had given Mary a gold necklace and heart pendant for her birthday several months before we parted company, but one night a few days before I dropped over with my letter she had a dream in which she lost her gold necklace and pendant, and she panicked; but that was her inner guiding principle preparing her for what was coming, and it lessened the pain of our parting considerably. But we both suffered all the same, and it wasn't until I read what Jesus said to

Jung's spiritual guide Philemon about suffering in Jung's *Red Book* that I begin to fathom the divine and merciful mystery of human suffering.

Life may well be a "hierarchy of devouring," but all of man's suffering serves the evolutionary purpose of our becoming; because through suffering we transform the consciousness of our *being* and *non-being* into the consciousness of our true self, which I had become very familiar with as I "worked" on myself with *conscious effort* and *intentional suffering* as I lived the secret way according to Gurdjieff's teaching, my *Royal Dictum*, and the sayings and parables of Jesus. And as preposterous as it may seem, **human suffering is nature's way of satisfying the longing in our soul to be all that we are meant to be**; that's the divine mystery of what Jesus meant when he appeared in Jung's garden…

It was noon on a hot summer day and Jung was taking a stroll in his garden at his home in Kusnacht by Lake Zurich. When he reached the shade of the high trees he saw his spiritual guide Philemon strolling in the fragrant grass. When Jung sought to approach him, he saw a blue shade come from the other side, and Philemon recognized the blue shade as Jesus, and after exchanging a few words Philemon brings Jung's experience in his garden to climactic resolution with the following revelation as he and Jesus speak:

"Recognize, Oh master and beloved, that your nature is also of the serpent," said Philemon to Jesus. "Were you not raised on the tree like a serpent? Have you laid aside your body, like the serpent its skin? Have you not practiced the healing arts, like the serpent? Did you not go to Hell before your ascent? And did you not see your brother there, who was shut away in the abyss?"

And the blue shade of Jesus replied: "You speak the truth. You are not lying. Even so, do you know what I bring you?"

"I know only one thing, that whoever hosts the worm also needs his brother," said Jung's spiritual guide Philemon. "What do you bring me, my beautiful guest? Lamentation and abomination were the gift of the worm. What will you give us?"

"I bring you the beauty of suffering. That is what is needed by whoever hosts the worm," replied Jesus. (*The Red Book*, A Reader's Edition, C. G. Jung, p.553)

Thus ends *The Red Book,* Jung's heroic journey of self-discovery; and when I read this I came to tears, because in those closing words by Jesus I saw through the divine mystery of human suffering and the unfathomable puzzle of life finally came together for me.

But it takes a long, long time for one to reach this point of spiritual clarity, and I wrote a spiritual musing for my blog (*December 26, 2015*) to part the veil of life and show what it takes to come to this critical point of discernment: —

Not Ready Yet...

*"All destiny leads down the same path—
growth, love and service."*

The Wheel of Life
A Memoir of Living and Dying
Elisabeth Kubler-Ross

Talking with a friend the other day, who over the summer holidays had read my book *The Lion that Swallowed Hemingway*, from which he gleaned a surprising insight into his own life, the topic of reincarnation came up and I told him about a dream I had that in my next life I'm going to come back as a precocious writer, and then I was about to share an epiphany I had about reincarnation but for some reason was censored and couldn't relate my epiphany because I couldn't remember it.

It's not unusual to have my mind censored when I'm talking with someone, and by being censored I don't mean that I had a "senior moment" or a "brain freeze," as they say today. It was certainly a lapse of memory, but it had nothing to do with brain chemistry; it had to do with the information I wasn't supposed to share with my friend because he wasn't meant to hear it. But who or what censored my thoughts?

As exciting as this may be, it's not the subject of today's spiritual musing; it is only my entry point, because it was this conversation that called me to write a musing on my epiphany on reincarnation which is as clear in my mind today as it was when it first came to me; and my epiphany is this: **no one can break the cycle of life and death until they are ready**, and making oneself ready was what inspired my epiphany on spiritual liberation; but before I reveal my epiphany, let me shed some light on this mystery of my mind going blank whenever I'm about to share something that is not meant to be shared with the person that I am speaking with.

This hasn't happened all that often, but enough times to alert me to my censor, and by censor I mean an inner guiding principle that is infinitely wiser than my working-day personality. And as strange as this may seem, I'm not alone in this unique relationship with my inner guiding principle because the Greek philosopher Socrates also had a censor that he called an inner voice, an "oracle which comes to me and always forbids me to do something which I am going to do, but never commands me to do anything," as he tells us in Plato's Dialogue the *Apology*.

I've never been commanded to do anything by my "oracle" either, but when I get censored I know I have been forbidden to share my thoughts with the person I'm speaking with, and I can only assume that it was either for my own protection or because it wasn't meant for them to hear what I was about to share. Why they weren't meant to hear what I was about to say, I can only guess; but the memory of what I wanted to share always comes back to me later after we have parted company. Now, back to my epiphany that I was called upon to share in today's spiritual musing…

I can't count the number of times in the course of my life that I've heard people say: *"This is my last life. I'm never coming back. One lifetime is enough for me, thank you,"* or some variation of this theme that one has had their fill of life and wants nothing more to do with it, and this includes people who believe in karma and reincarnation and should know better; but they don't, and that was my epiphany.

What I find curious however is why it took so long for me to see it, because I had long ago come to the realization in my journey of self-discovery that the purpose of our life is to become what we are meant to be, which is our true self; but herein lies the mystery of today's musing, because I know now why I was given this epiphany that I was about to share with my friend the other day before I got censored.

Gurdjieff impressed upon me that nature will only evolve man so far and no further, and to become what we are meant to be we have to take evolution into our own hands with *conscious effort* and *intentional suffering*; this is why I was censored when speaking with my friend. My epiphany would have threatened the spirit of the status quo, which evolves unconsciously through the natural process of karma and reincarnation until one has evolved enough to take evolution into their own hands and consciously complete what nature cannot finish, as I was compelled to do early in my life when I was called to find my true self, and my friend was so firmly entrenched in the comfortable complacency of the status quo that my epiphany would have threatened his self-image, which is why I was censored.

Upon reflection, I can't help but see a common thread now running through all the times that I got censored; and that common thread is what Carl Jung called "the problem of resistance to understanding." In a letter to his friend and pupil Doctor Hans Schmid (*November 6, 1915*), Jung revealed how man's resistance to understanding was finally clarified for him by a vision given to Brigitta of Sweden (1303-1373), who became St. Bridget. Jung wrote that Brigitta's vision explained the psychology of devils, which in Jung's lexicon would be the psychology of man's unconscious shadow self that is insatiable in its appetite for life experience.

"Their belly is so swollen because their greed was boundless, for they filled themselves and were not sated, and so great was their greed that, had they been able to gain the whole world, they would gladly have exerted themselves, and would moreover have desired to reign in heaven," wrote Brigitta about her vision; and Jung realized that "the devil (the shadow side of our ego personality) is the devourer," and "understanding is likewise a devouring," because "understanding swallows you up."

This was such a powerful vision that Jung immediately saw why people (especially his patients who bared their soul to him) have a resistance to understanding. "Understanding is a fearfully bounding power, at times a veritable murderer of the soul as soon as it flattens out vitally important differences," wrote Jung in his letter. "The core of the individual is a mystery of life, which is snuffed out when it is 'grasped.'" Hence man's resistance to understanding: our shadow does not want to be snuffed out and swallowed up by being understood and resists the light of cognition; but this is such a profound insight that it needs further explanation...

Our shadow is the unconscious side of our ego personality, the repository of everything that we do not want to deal with consciously; like those embarrassing little moments when we made a fool of ourselves with our friends or at a social function, or the lie that we told to save face and countless other sins and foibles and grotesqueries that we refuse to resolve by dealing with them consciously and which over time coalesce into little matrixes of negative energy that become our personal demons. This is why I refuted John Irving's karmically flawed premise in my spiritual musing "Chicken Little Syndrome," his personal belief central to all his novels. "You don't choose your demons, they choose you," he boasted, with authorial certainty; a totally blind perspective on how the logic of life works.

Karma is a personal responsibility, and not until we have evolved enough through the natural process of karma and reincarnation will we be spiritually mature enough to take evolution into our own hands and live our life with conscious karmic awareness; that's why I was censored from sharing my epiphany with my friend the other day, because the thought of taking karmic responsibility for one's own life scares the devil out of people, and one instinctively blocks out the light of understanding by going into denial to protect their shadow, and my friend was spared this shock by the omniscient guiding principle of my censor because he wasn't ready to hear it.

And this brings me back to the central motif of my spiritual musing: **no one can break the cycle of life and death until they are ready to take evolution into their own hands.** Which begs the question: when is one ready?

Given the analogy of the oyster creating its own precious pearl, man creates his own precious spiritual identity by individuating the consciousness of his many personalities that he created with every incarnation. This presupposes reincarnation, because it's not possible to individuate one's spiritual identity in one lifetime alone; and I have proof of this from my own past-life regressions which I've written about in *The Summoning of Noman* and need not expound upon here.

The Oyster's pearl grows out of the oyster's own cells, and our spiritual identity grows out of the karmic "cells" of our many life experiences, which means that we grow in positive and negative karma until we have grown as far as evolution can take us; but like the acorn seed that longs to become an oak tree, so too do we long to become all that we are meant to be, and to do this we have to take evolution into our own hands to complete what nature cannot finish, and herein lies our quandary.

To complete what nature cannot finish we have to resolve our negative karma, because the consciousness of negative karma is not pure enough for our soul self to realize its divine nature; and to purify the consciousness of our negative karmic self we have to transform it, which is the essential purpose of all spiritual teachings. But how exactly do we transform our negative karmic self?

I began the process of self-transformation with Gurdjieff's teaching of "work on oneself" with *conscious effort* and *intentional suffering,* which inspired my edict of self-denial that I called my *Royal Dictum,* which in turn awakened me to the secret way that I found in Christ's sayings and parables, and the more I practiced the secret way the more I transformed my negative karmic self; and *by secret way I mean the art of purifying the consciousness of my negative karmic self by becoming a giver instead of a taker, which was the most difficult part of my journey of self-discovery.*

In the words of St. Paul, I practiced the art of "dying daily" to my selfish nature and disciplined myself to become unselfish. That's how I purified the consciousness of my negative karmic self, which Socrates confirmed in the *Phaedo*: "And what is purification but the separation of the soul from the body, as I was saying before, the habit of the soul gathering and collecting herself into herself."

That's how one takes evolution into their own hands, by becoming a giver and not a taker; because the act of unselfish living has the power to purify the consciousness of our negative karmic self and, in the words of Jesus, makes our two selves into one self which he called "the pearl of great price."

Given my love for aphorisms, I distilled my whole journey of self-discovery into a simple saying which speaks to the paradoxical process of spiritual self-realization consciousness: **the more you give of yourself, the more of yourself you will have to give; and conversely, the less you give of yourself, the less of yourself you will have to give.** And one day we will have grown enough to realize our spiritual identity, as I did that day in my mother's kitchen when I gave birth to my spiritual self. I *knew* that I was immortal, and the longing in my soul no longer drove my *will to be* because I had *become* my true self.

Not until we have evolved enough to give back to life then will we be ready to break the cycle of life and death, because this is the only way we can complete what nature cannot finish; and until we do, we karmically fate ourselves to return to life to complete our journey of self-discovery. This is what I couldn't tell my friend the other day, because my "oracle" knew that silence was the better part of wisdom.

———

"I bring you the beauty of suffering. That is what is needed by whoever hosts the worm," said Jesus to Jung's guide Philemon, which was Christ's way of telling us that suffering keeps the "worm" in man from growing, and the "worm" is man's shadow, the unresolved side of our ego personality that keeps man from transcending himself; but this is such a sacred mystery that to bring it into the light of day only risks profaning it…

13. THE THREE CIRCLES OF LIFE

"Man is a stream whose source is hidden..."

Consider three concentric circles, with each circle representing a spectrum of life; the large outer circle being the *Exoteric Circle of Life*, the smaller middle circle the *Mesoteric Circle of Life*, and the smallest inner circle the *Esoteric Circle of Life,* and together they make up man's evolutionary journey through the entire spectrum of the life process....

When I dropped out of university to forge my own path in life with Gurdjieff's teaching of "work on oneself," I vowed to build my life upon the truth of my own experiences, because I had painfully come to see that this was the only truth that I could trust; and experience by experience, the truth of my life began to grow into my own personal worldview.

I've always regretted not having a personal mentor, someone I could talk to when I needed guidance; but over time I came to see that it was much better for me to forge my own path in life, because this gave me the confidence to trust my own experiences, like my seven past-life regressions which cleared up the mystery of my earlier experience of going back in time and witnessing the inception of life on Planet Earth, an experience that made no sense to me at all until I experienced myself as an atom of God in the Body of God and the actual dawning of my reflective self-consciousness in my first primordial human lifetime.

It took a long time to connect these two experiences—the genesis of life on Planet Earth and my regression to the Body of God where all souls come from, and it worked in my favor to not have had a personal mentor to talk this over with because he might have suggested that I see a psychiatrist; but I did not have a mentor, and upon the basis of my experiences, as hard to believe as they may be, I came to see the divine archetypal pattern of soul's journey from God and through life and back to God again, which solved the puzzle of life for me.

What made my experience so unique was not that I experienced myself as an atom of God in the Body of God, which many mystics and poets have experienced, but that I experienced myself as a soul without self-consciousness. Just as an infant is born without a sense of self, which it acquires as it grows from day to day, so too was I sent into the world without a sense of self; and as my embryonic soul evolved through the process of natural evolution, it acquired its own identity, as Keats had discerned in his letter to his brother which he titled "The Vale of Soul Making." In effect, Keats saw the mystery of soul's journey through what he called "a medium of a world like this," and I *experienced* this mystery.

And because I was a writer who grew to trust my creative instinct, I learned to piece together the puzzling pieces of our becoming, as I did in my spiritual musing "The Tumbler of Life" in which I try to resolve the mystery of our perfect and imperfect nature; but before I quote my musing, let me share my insight into *The Three Circles of Life...*

Given the logic of my three experiences (1, experiencing the genesis of life on Planet Earth; 2, experiencing myself as an embryonic soul with group consciousness but no self-consciousness in the Body of God; and 3, experiencing the dawning of my reflective self-consciousness in my first primordial human lifetime as a higher primate), and then the fourth and final experience which connected all of these experiences to give me the big picture of the Divine Plan of God, which was the experience of my own immortal nature in my mother's kitchen that fateful day, when I put them all together they created the three stages of our evolution through life—*the Exoteric, Mesoteric, and Esoteric Circles of Life*.

When I experienced the genesis of life on Planet Earth, I experienced myself as Soul imbuing the first building blocks of life (the amino acids that the vaporous gases from the earth and sky created when they combined); but as I later deduced, it was not me personally that had imbued the amino acids with the creative vital life force of Soul, it was the "I Am" consciousness of Divine Spirit (the Body of God), which then evolved through the life process from the lowest life form to the life form of a higher primate where I as a nascent soul experienced the dawning of my reflective self-consciousness in my first primordial human lifetime. And from lifetime to lifetime, I continued to evolve in my reflective self-consciousness until the natural laws of karma and reincarnation could evolve me no further, and I had to take evolution into my own hands with *conscious effort* and *intentional suffering* to complete what nature could not finish, and I realized my immortal self in my mother's kitchen that summer day while she was kneading bread dough on the kitchen table.

In my evolution up the ladder of life, up to and including my first primordial human lifetime and many more lifetimes after that, I finally began to have a sense of my own immortal soul, which I did in my lifetime as Solomon the Good Slave, and which I came to see as the *exoteric,* or first stage of evolution of life where Soul (the "I Am" consciousness of God) is driven by its own divine imperative to grow and evolve through the life process for the encoded purpose of realizing its divine nature; and as I grew in my reflective self-consciousness through karma and reincarnation, I acquired my own identity enough to want to know **who I was,** which I took very seriously in my current lifetime; that's why I went on my spiritual quest to find my true self or die trying, and happily I succeeded.

When life evolves one to the point where they take the question **"who am I?"** very seriously and try to answer it by seeking for an answer in the world's religions, philosophies, and literature (this is the stage that I came to see as the *mesoteric*, or second stage of evolution through life), and one will evolve through the *mesoteric* stage until they have realized enough life experience to gravitate to the *esoteric* stage of evolution, which can only happen when one has acquired enough identity and the mesoteric stage can do no more for them and one becomes so desperate to satisfy the longing in their soul for wholeness that *the merciful law of divine synchronicity* intercedes to open one up to the sacred knowledge of the secret way, as I experienced when Gurdjieff's teaching came into my life by way of Ouspensky's book *In Search of the Miraculous*.

But this isn't to say that *the merciful law of divine synchronicity* only comes to our assistance when we are so desperate that we will do anything to satisfy the longing in our soul, because it is always opening doors for us—if we are ready to enter and take the risk, because if there is one thing that I have learned about *the omniscient guiding principle of life* it is that every experience we have in life can be an entry into the *esoteric* stage of evolution where we can satisfy the longing in our soul for wholeness and completeness. And having said this, I can now share my spiritual musing that speaks to the natural process of evolution through the *exoteric* and *mesoteric* stages of life that makes us ready to take evolution into our own hands and be initiated into the *esoteric* stage of evolution: —

The Tumbler of Life

"Behold, be grateful, and forgive that which you did not understand or control. For life is divine, it is perfect, and it naturally manifests the will of its creator," said Jesus in Glenda Green's book, *Love without End, Jesus Speaks*, the true story of Glenda Green's experience painting the portrait of Jesus who appeared to her over several months to have his portrait painted for reasons that her book explains; but it took me a few years of serious reflection and creative writing to absorb the wisdom of Christ's comment.

Love without End, Jesus Speaks was recommended by St. Padre Pio during one of my spiritual healing sessions with the gifted psychic who channeled the humble saint, and which I explored in my novel *Healing with Padre Pio*; but it wasn't until I was given the image of a rock tumbler polisher long after I read the book for the second or third time that Christ's words of life being divine and perfect called out to be explored in today's spiritual musing, but I am writing this musing under protest because I know where it is going. But before I abandon to my creative unconscious to explore the paradigm-shifting wisdom of Christ's comment in today's spiritual musing, let me get something out of the way first.

It goes without saying that many readers will question the authenticity of my experience with St. Padre Pio, perhaps less so than the reality of Glenda Green's miraculous experience with

THE MERCIFUL LAW OF DIVINE SYNCHRONICITY

Jesus Christ (her book *Love without End, Jesus Speaks* and her portrait *The Lamb and the Lion* are very hard to dismiss, regardless how skeptical one may be); but as I've come to realize, life is an individual journey of self-discovery, and what we believe depends entirely upon our need to know.

I had a very strong need to know what Jesus said in Glenda Green's book, that's why Padre Pio recommended the book for me to read; and although I went into the book with some reservations about the reality of Glenda Green's experience, the more I read what Jesus said to her while she painted his portrait, the more I believed in the authenticity of her experience because what Jesus said to her was what was left out of the Gospels, and I couldn't read the book fast enough because it satisfied my need to know the hidden part of Christ's teaching that he could not reveal to the public because the world was not ready to hear it.

"And the disciples came, and said unto him, Why speakest thou unto them in parables?

"He answered and said unto them, *Because it is given unto you to know the mysteries of the kingdom of heaven, but to them it is not given. For whosoever hath, to him shall be given, and he shall have more abundance; but whosoever hath not, from him shall be taken even that he hath*" (Matthew 13: 10-12).

Jesus is speaking in code, saying quite simply that there is a natural law of attraction that works in the life of man which has been expressed in popular sayings like, "much gathers more," "it takes money to make money," "nothing succeeds like success," "birds of a feather flock together," "misery loves company," and many similar gems of wisdom all reflecting the hidden law of life that has been exploited in self-help books by those that have discovered how this law of attraction works, like *The Secret* by Rhonda Byrne; but unless one understands the context of what Jesus said about the law of attraction, one will never appreciate the wisdom of Christ's teaching of salvation, and the context of Christ's teaching is the **secret way**, which is the underlying theme of today's spiritual musing.

The question that no one can answer unless they have broken the code of the **secret way** in Christ's teaching, is this: what did Christ's disciples have that Jesus could give them more of what they had so they could know the mysteries of the kingdom of heaven? What was this mysterious quality that his disciples had that made them worthy of the sacred knowledge that Jesus shared with them in private?

"Many are called but few are chosen," said Jesus, speaking to this mysterious quality that his disciples had; and when all is said and done, this mysterious quality that his disciples had was enough spiritual gravitas to attract them to the **secret way**, and by spiritual gravitas I mean the individuated consciousness of life experience.

"Nature will only evolve man so far, and no further," said Gurdjieff, who called his radical teaching of self-transformation "esoteric Christianity," and the natural process of individuation through karma and reincarnation had evolved Christ's disciples as far as it could take them, and they were ready to take evolution into their own hands to complete what nature could not finish; that's why they gravitated to the sacred knowledge of the **secret way** in Christ's teaching.

In Christ's words, they were called by life and chosen by Jesus to receive the sacred knowledge of the **secret way** that would complete what they could not finish through more life experience, which was to realize their divine nature (which Jesus called "kingdom of heaven"); and how they were made ready is the subject of today's spiritual musing...

Jesus alludes to it but never made it clear in the Gospels that we live more than one lifetime, but in his talks with Glenda Green he explained the mystery of reincarnation: *"Your immortality is a simple thing, and so your understanding will be more accurate if you keep it simple as well. By the will of God, life creates a place for you infinitely again and again, according to your love and in relation to your loved ones. The philosophy of reincarnation is not that simple. It does affirm your continuity, and that is good. However, there's a twist in it which defers your immortality back to structure and linearity, which is not true. Your immortality is not imprisoned within a wheel of life, or pathway of cause and effect. Neither are you the product of linear evolvement. You were created in perfection, and perfect love, and you do* **continue** *to re-manifest infinitely, but it is according to the will of the Father, and according to your own purposes, your own love, and your own place of service and learning. You actually only have one life! It's just a very long one, with many chapters"* (Love without End, Jesus Speaks, by Glenda Green, pp. 76-77).

Jesus let the cat out of the bag. He revealed that reincarnation is a fact of life, but not the way the world has come to understands it.

Reincarnation is not linear, which I learned from St. Padre Pio when he told me that I chose to live my same life over again to achieve a different outcome; meaning, I chose to be reborn into my same body because I was not satisfied with what I had done with my first lifetime as Orest Stocco, which I explored in my memoir *The Summoning of Noman*; and I did achieve what I intended to achieve in my current parallel life, which was to find my true self that I wrote about in *The Pearl of Great Price,* so I know from my own life that what Jesus said about reincarnation is true, and whether anyone believes this or not will depend entirely upon their need to know.

I've gone into great personal detail in my two memoirs on how I found my true self, but to bring resolution to today's spiritual musing it behooves me to explain how I acquired that mysterious quality that attracted me to the sacred knowledge of the **secret way**; and by mysterious quality I mean that certain energy of the individuated consciousness of life that Jesus called "virtue."

I acquired enough "virtue" by living Gurdjieff's teaching of "work on oneself," my personal edict of self-denial which I called my *Royal Dictum* (for three and a half years I denied myself the pleasures of life, sex being the most difficult to deny but most rewarding in "virtue"), and the sayings of Jesus which went a long way to helping me transform the consciousness of my lower self and making my two selves into one; and the more "virtue" that I acquired, the more the **secret way** opened up to me—which is what Jesus meant with his saying *"For whosoever hath, to him shall be given, and he shall have more abundance."*

But it wasn't until I realized that the surest way of acquiring "virtue" was by simply living a life of virtue, with specific emphasis upon the virtue of goodness which Socrates deemed to be the most noble, all of which cultivated **a conscious attitude of giving to life instead of taking from life** (honesty, fairness, and truthfulness were not easy virtues to live by when one is in business for himself, and they cost me dearly in more ways than one), that I begin to resolve the mystery of the **secret way**; and the more "virtue" that I acquired, the more I *became* my true self. That's how I realized that one cannot find one's true self as such, but must *become* one's true self...

I can now return to the image of the rock tumbler polisher that came to me when I thought of Jesus's comment about life being divine and perfect, which was my inspiration for today's spiritual musing, because for the longest time I wanted to write a musing on Jesus's comment but couldn't reconcile man's imperfect nature with his comment that life was divine and perfect because both were true.

I *knew* that man is an imperfect/perfect being, but not until my unconscious offered me the image of the rock tumbler polisher did I see through the mystery of man's paradoxical nature that Jesus alludes to in Glenda's book when he speaks of man's assured continuity according to God's will and man's own volition.

"You were created in perfection, and perfect love, and you do **continue** *to re-manifest infinitely, but it is according to the will of the Father, and according to your own purposes, your own love, and your own place of service and learning,"* said Jesus; but I would never have understood what Jesus meant by this had I not had my past-life regression to the Body of God where all new

souls come from and my regression to my first primordial human lifetime when I gave birth to a new "I" of God (my own reflective self-consciousness, as rudimentary as it was), because this experience confirmed that we are all immortal souls pre-destined by our own divine nature (*"God's will,"* as Jesus said) to realize our true self through the natural process of karma and reincarnation (*"according to your own purposes, your own love, and your own place of service and learning,"* said Jesus), which I confirmed with my other past-life regressions until I was evolved enough to take evolution into my own hands and realize my true self, which I did in my current lifetime.

This is how I resolved the paradox of our imperfect/perfect nature, and the image of the rock tumbler polisher symbolizes the natural process of karmic evolution through life, because like a rock tumbler that polishes the rocks of all their rough edges and makes them sooth and perfect, so does the tumbler of life pit us all against each other to wear off our karmic imperfections.

Unfortunately, as we are all forced to see when we can no longer bear the burden of our own bitterness and sorrow, the tumbler of life cannot wear off our karmic imperfections enough for us to realize the purpose of our existence, and to complete what nature cannot finish we are compelled by the imperative of our own divine nature to take evolution into our own hands and acquire enough "virtue" to *become* our true self; only then will we see that life is divine and perfect in all of its imperfections.

I cannot expect anyone to believe that I had these experiences that allowed me to work out the meaning and purpose of life, but the logic of our becoming that was born of my incredible experiences answered the three imponderable questions of my life: *who am I? why am I?* and *where did I come from?* And that's good enough for me…

14. THE ONLY WAY OUT OF LIFE IS THROUGH LIFE

"Life is a prison...."

For argument's sake, let's say that what I experienced did happen to me; I did *actually* experience the genesis of life on Planet Earth; and I did *actually* experience myself as an atom of God in the Body of God, with no reflective self-consciousness; and I did *actually* experience the dawning of my reflective self-consciousness in my first primordial human lifetime as a higher primate; and I did *actually* experience the birth of my immortal self in my mother's kitchen that day—let's say this all *actually* happened to me; wouldn't my journey from the Body of God through the evolutionary process of life and on up to the birth of my spiritual self be the archetypal pattern of every soul's journey? And if so, wouldn't this shed light on the puzzling comment that Socrates made in Plato's *Phaedo?*

"There is a doctrine uttered in secret that man is a prisoner who has no right to open the door of his prison and run away," said Socrates, a doctrine that he said he did not quite understand; but Socrates understood the secret doctrine well enough to offer us a key to the door of man's prison, a key that will free the soul from the prison of one's life.

How Socrates came upon the sacred knowledge of the secret way of life, I can only speculate and say that he was called to the secret way because he was ready to be initiated into the *Esoteric Circle of Life*; but given what I experienced in my own journey of self-discovery and liberation from the prison of my own life, what Socrates said about escaping from the prison of one's life resonates perfectly well with me.

"And what is purification but the separation of the soul from the body, as I was saying before; the habit of soul gathering and collecting herself into herself, out of all the courses of the body; and dwelling in her own place, as in another life, so also in this, as far as she can; the release of the soul from the chains of the body?" said

Socrates in the *Phaedo;* which confirms what Jesus said about spiritual liberation from the prison of one's life in his most paradoxical and difficult saying: ***"He that loveth his life shall lose it; and he that hateth his life in this world shall keep it unto life eternal"*** (John 12: 25).

Socrates, Jesus; these are no ordinary people, and what they said about life has to be taken seriously. The problem the world has however is interpreting what they said, because they both revealed the sacred knowledge of the secret way in their own idiom, which has led to a lot of confusion. But what if one had a key that would unlock the mystery of the sacred knowledge of the secret way? Would that help to resolve the confusion?

In my heart, I'd like to believe it would; but experience has proven that this is not possible because life is an individual journey, and not until one has been made ready by life will one even begin to "hear" the silent voice of the secret way. So it doesn't matter what Socrates, Jesus, or any initiate of the *Esoteric Circle of Life* has to say about liberating one's soul from the prison of life, the sacred knowledge will only be appreciated by those who can "hear" it—but no one knows who that person will be! And so I shall continue with the story of my incredible relationship with *the merciful law of divine synchronicity...*

As easy as it may be to believe that life is merciless, cruel, and unkind— "a hierarchy of devouring"—my own journey of self-discovery has led me to believe that life is what it is, *an enantiodromiac process of becoming,* both cruel and kind, that facilitates our individuation through life; and without the conflict that arises out of the opposing forces of life (good and evil, right and wrong, light and darkness, love and hate, cruelty and kindness), we would never grow and evolve enough to realize our divine nature.

Unfortunately, one has to go through all the emotions that man is forced to experience as he goes through the *enantiodromiac process of life* before he realizes that life is, as Shakespeare tells us, "neither good nor bad but thinking makes it so," and by the time this happens one will be ready for the secret way of life that will complete one's destined purpose of wholeness and completeness; and that's when one begins to notice all the assistance that one receives from *the merciful law of divine synchronicity.*

"Synchronicity is an ever present reality for those who have eyes to see," said Jung, who coined the term "synchronicity" to conceptualize the experience of a "meaningful coincidence," but not until one connects synchronicity with *the omniscient guiding principle of life* will one grasp the impenetrable mystery of the synchronicity principle, which brings me to the heart of my story—the "I Am" consciousness of God.

If, as I experienced when I went back through time to the genesis of life on Planet Earth, Soul is the "I Am" consciousness of God that animates the life process for the purpose of individuating the "I Am" consciousness of God until Soul realizes its divine nature through the process of the natural evolution of life, as I also experienced with my past-life regressions to the Body of God where all souls come from and through the life process to the dawning of my reflective self consciousness in my first primordial human lifetime as a higher primate and from lifetime to lifetime until I experienced the birth of my spiritual self in my mother's kitchen when I took evolution into my own hands to complete what nature could not finish, wouldn't it be logical to conclude that this whole drama of life is directed by the "I Am" consciousness of God that I have called *the omniscient guiding principle of life?*

Unless I dismiss my life story as some kind of ongoing elaborate psychic fantasy, I have no choice but to accept the logic of my own self-individuation as I experienced it; and, in all honesty, after all the reading that I have done and different paths that I have lived in my efforts to answer the driving questions of my life (*who am I?* and *why am I?*), I have to accept the conclusion of my quest for my true self—whether it be fantasy or not; and my conclusion is that we are all assisted by *an omniscient guiding principle* in our journey through life, whether we see it or not—but always, I hasten to add, in accordance with our free will!

And this is where I part company with the teachings of the world that try to short-circuit the process of our *becoming*—like Christianity for example, which proffers salvation through the death of Jesus Christ upon the cross; and Buddhism, which proffers the non-existence of our soul self by claiming that we are all one Self with no individual identity; and the New Age Religion of the Light and Sound of God which also proffers the belief that we are Soul and don't know it, without offering the other half of the self-realization process that Jesus called making the two into one and Socrates called soul "gathering and collecting herself into herself." Simply stated, there are no shortcuts to one's true self as these teachings proffer; that's what my journey of self-discovery revealed to me, and what a relief it was to see through the fog of these teachings that try to short-circuit the individuation of our soul self.

This is why I was attracted to teachings that opened me up to the secret way, because the law of attraction demands that "much gathers more," and the more "virtue" that I realized living my *Royal Dictum*, Gurdjieff's teaching of "work on oneself," and the sayings of Jesus, the more I pulled into my energy field literature that resonated with my path of self-discovery, like Rumi's mystical poetry and C. G. Jung's psychology of individuation.

"This life is the way, the long sought-after way to the unfathomable, which we call divine. There is no other way, all other ways are false paths," said Jung in *The Red Book;* but as obvious as this insight may appear to be, it is so profound that it may take a lifetime to see that life is both our prison and the way out of our prison—the greatest irony of our life.

But good God, it took a long time to solve this mystery! I knew that I was a prisoner of my own personality. The traumatic sexual experience that catapulted me into my quest for my true self awakened me to my shadow self, and I had to find my true self or die trying; that's why I was attracted to teachings like Gurdjieff's "work on oneself," because by "working" on myself I could transform the consciousness of my shadow and realize my true self—as Jesus promised with his teaching of making the two into one. This is why I can be so categorical in my understanding that we cannot short-circuit the individuation process like Christianity, Buddhism, and that New Age Religion of the Light and Sound of God try to do.

The simple truth is that life is both our prison and our salvation, but the secret of our salvation lies in knowing how to live our life so that we can liberate ourselves from the prison of our life. And it doesn't matter how we slice the cake, Socrates had it right by offering us the key to our prison door in his philosophy of virtue, because when push comes to shove the only way to transcend our life is by transforming the consciousness of our unresolved lower self by living a life of virtue. This is why I concluded that the fundamental purpose of life is to simply be a good person, because **being a good person initiates the process of self-resolution that makes our two selves into one**; and in the fullness of time one will realize their true self and liberate themselves from the prison of life.

This was the concluding resolution of my book *Death, the Final Frontier* that I was called upon to write while working on this book (*a resolution, I might add, that was brought about by an extraordinary synchronicity!*), and not until I finished writing it did I see why I was called away from this book, because as terrifying as it may be to face our final hour, the point of my book *Death, the Final Frontier* was to offer as much proof as I possibly could that our life does not end when our body dies, that there is a continuum to our life that never ends; and it is the purpose of this book to offer as much proof as I possibly can to show that we are guided through life by a *benevolent guiding principle,* which brings me to my next chapter on some remarkable coincidences that I have experienced and read about that shore up my conviction that life is an *enantiodromiac process* both cruel and kind that individuates the consciousness of our soul self, a natural dynamic of personal growth that is assisted by *the merciful law of divine synchronicity*— "an ever present reality for those who have eyes to see," as C. G. Jung realized in his own journey of self-discovery…

15. SOME REMARKABLE COINCIDENCES

"Synchronicity comes along to wake us and fulfill us..."

"Synchronicity is a mind-boggling and sometimes eerie rendezvous between the world and our inner selves," said David Richo in his book *The Power of Coincidence*, subtitled *How Life Shows Us What We Need to Know*; and I don't think anyone would disagree with this description of what I have come to recognize as *the merciful law of divine synchronicity*, because we've all had meaningful coincidences that have boggled our mind.

But not until we understand why the "synchronicity principle," as Jung called it, comes into play in our life will we ever make sense of why we were blessed to have a synchronicity experience that changed the course of our life, like I did when I was given Ouspensky's book *In Search of the Miraculous* that introduced me to G. I. Gurdjieff, and like the experience that Frank N. McMillan Jr. had one day in a country store café with an eccentric artist who introduced him to the name Carl Jung, as Frank N. McMillan III tells us in his book *Finding Jung: Frank N. McMillan Jr., A Life in Quest of the Lion*.

Seven-year-old Frank N. McMillan Jr. had a disturbing dream of a powerful, majestic lion that haunted him all of his life until quite by "chance" one day he met an eccentric artist in a country store café "ecstatically waving a letter in the air as he shouted out: 'He wrote back to me!'" And after the man had calmed down, Frank asked: "Who wrote back to you?" And the man replied: "Carl Jung from Switzerland." And Frank responded, "Who's that?"

"Jung is a master psychologist, a soul doctor, an esteemed writer, and one of the greatest healers of all time. Just read his books," replied the eccentric artist, and such an impression did that abstract expressionist painter and eccentric recluse, whose name was Forrest Bess, make upon Frank McMillan, who was in the throes of a mid-life crisis, that he followed up on the man's advice and read the *Collected Works* of C. G. Jung who pulled him so deeply into his psychology of individuation that Frank McMillan "attributed his rebirth and becoming his 'true self' to Carl Jung," and he loved to say, "Jung saved my life."

That may sound absurd to anyone who has not experienced a loss of personal meaning and purpose and doesn't know how to find their way out of their despair, which many people fall into when they have a mid-life crisis—Dante expressed it best when he wrote in his *Inferno*: "In the middle of the journey of our life / I found myself in a dark wood, / For I had lost the right path," but when "life shows us what we need to know," as David Richo expresses the synchronicity principle, we can tune in with life again, as Frank McMillan did when Forrest Bess introduced him to the name Carl Jung whose psychology of individuation put him on the path to his true self; so we can understand why Frank McMillan would say "Jung saved my life," because in a way he did.

When I came back from France where I had gone to begin my quest for my true self, I went to university to study philosophy in the hope that the "mother of all disciplines" would put me on the right path to my true self, but instead philosophy pulled me out into a sea of endless dialectics and I feared getting lost and drowning; and that's when Gurdjieff came into my life by way of Ouspensky's book *In Search of the Miraculous* that changed the course of my life; so I can resonate with Frank McMillan's comment about Jung saving his life, because without Gurdjieff's teaching I would probably be still out there looking for the path to my true self. And this brings me to my rather unique perspective on *the merciful law of divine synchronicity*, which speaks to our dual consciousness and destined purpose.

Everyone who has written a book on synchronicity has caught a glimpse of *the omniscient guiding principle of life*— "…synchronicity is a spiritual event, one that shows the unity of human, natural, and divine reality," says David Richo in *The Power of Coincidence*, and Phil Cousineau writes in his book *Soul Moments*: "…synchronicity is a soul moment, an electrifying experience, as sudden as a visitation by a god, a palpable inrush of grace and power, one of the defining moments in life, a sudden conviction that we might be moved beyond fate and realize a hint of our destiny," and Robert H. Hopcke gives us an insight into the synchronicity principle that conceptualizes what I experienced in my own journey of self-discovery in his book *There*

THE MERCIFUL LAW OF DIVINE SYNCHRONICITY

Are No Accidents: "...our lives have a narrative structure, like that of novels, and at those moments we call synchronistic this structure is brought to our awareness in a way that has a significant impact on our lives."

All three authors imply a divine agency at work with the synchronicity principle; Richo calling synchronicity a "spiritual event," Cousineau calling synchronicity a "soul moment," and Hopcke pointing to our destined purpose by suggesting that our lives have an inherent narrative structure like a novel that is impacted by the synchronicity principle—but despite their intuitive glimpse of this *omniscient guiding principle,* none of these authors (nor anyone else, that I am aware of) have connected enough dots to see the big picture of the Divine Plan of God as I experienced it with my own journey of self-discovery; and as mystifying as it may be, I trust my own story enough to say quite categorically that we are all guided through life by a merciful and benevolent agency to help us realize our destined purpose.

If I may quote Phil Cousineau again, what he said about synchronicity would be a perfect entry into my perspective on the Divine Plan of God. He said that synchronicity is *"one of the defining moments in life, a sudden conviction that we might be moved beyond* ***fate*** *and realize a hint of our **destiny**,"* This is how I felt about Gurdjieff's teaching—an inner conviction that it would save me from myself, despite not grasping the imperative of the secret way implicit to his teaching which I did once I began living my *Royal Dictum.*

Fate and **destiny**, these are the twin forces in our life that cause us so much heartache and confusion, and not until we understand the dynamic of these two forces will we find peace of mind and resolution; which is what I managed to do in my journey of self-discovery with the assistance of *the merciful law of divine synchronicity...*

If I hadn't experienced what I did when I went back through time to the genesis of life on Planet Earth and my past-life regression to the Body of God and dawning of my reflective self-consciousness and finally the birth of my immortal self, I would never have resolved the issue of our karmic fate, which we create ourselves by the life we live, and our destined purpose which we are born with because we are atoms of God encoded to realize our divine nature, because our karmic fate is determined by our own free will and our destined purpose is pre-determined by our encoded divine nature and **our karmic fate is not always in agreement with our destined purpose**—the very issue that causes us so much heartache and confusion that *the merciful law of divine synchronicity* helps us to resolve!

When I came back from France where I had gone to begin my quest for my true self I was inspired to go to university to study philosophy, which led to my serendipitous discovery of Gurdjieff's teaching that put me on the right path to my true self; but what inspired me to go to university? I had no knowledge of Gurdjieff, but he was what I needed to get me on the right path to my true self just as Frank McMillan who had no knowledge of Carl Jung needed him to get him on his right path. But—*and this is the BUT that opens the door to the mystery of our destined purpose!* —had not *the merciful law of divine synchronicity* interceded to help Frank McMillan and myself find the right path to our true self, we would probably have floundered until the variables of our life favorably converged once more to allow for the synchronicity principle to come to our assistance and satisfy our deepest longing.

Synchronicities don't just happen out of the blue, even though they appear to do so; they are the symbolic manifestation of the meaningful convergence of our **inner need** with **outer events** of our life—like my inner need for the right path to find my true self and the meaningful convergence of outer events (going to university to study philosophy where I met the student who was "nudged" to buy Ouspensky's book *In Search of the Miraculous* to give to me, not knowing if I knew anything about Gurdjieff's teaching or not), and Frank McMillan's inner need for a way out of his mid-life crisis that would give his life more meaning and purpose and going into that country grocery store café where he serendipitously met an eccentric artist who introduced him to Carl Jung who "saved" his life.

Were these chance occurrences, or divinely choreographed? Was I inspired to go to university to study philosophy because on some deep unconscious level I *knew* that I would find the path that would take me to my true self, just as Frank McMillan *knew* on some deep unconscious level that he would find the path to his true self by going into that country store café for lunch where he met Forrest Bess who introduced him to Carl Jung, or did Frank McMillan and I just happen by chance to be at the right place at the right time?

When one has experienced as many meaningful coincidences as I have, one would be inclined to favor providential guidance over random chance, which I do; and to make my case I'm going to relate one remarkable coincidence that I experienced which sealed my belief that we are all guided by a *benevolent guiding principle*, and whether we call it God, God within, our Higher Self, Inner Master, Providence, or Divine Spirit does not matter; all that matters is that this guidance comes by some all-knowing benevolent agency, such as the synchronicity principle. (It may come by way of dreams, meeting the love of our life by "chance," and so on; *the omniscient guiding principle of life* is always there to help us find our way.)

However, before I relate my incredible coincidence I'm obliged to explain how I came to resolve the unique relationship that we have with our destined purpose, and I say "unique" because **we have free will and our destined purpose is pre-scripted**, which means that we are not always in agreement with our destined purpose and are in conflict with ourselves.

As I experienced in my regression, I came into the world from the Body of God as an atom of God's Body without a reflective self-consciousness, and I was sent into the world to evolve through life to grow and individuate the creative life force (the "I Am" consciousness of Soul) for the destined purpose of creating a new "I" of God and realizing my divine nature, which I also experienced when I gave birth to my reflective self-consciousness in my first primordial human lifetime as a higher primate which evolved from incarnation to incarnation until I gave birth to my immortal self in my mother's kitchen in my current life; and I can only assume that my journey of individuation is the same archetypal journey that every soul experiences through life—an assumption that world literature bears witness to, like Rumi's mystical poetry, the Taoist text *The Secret of the Golden Flower*, and Jung's psychology of individuation to name a few examples.

When all the dust has settled, this means that as we evolve through life under the aegis of karma and reincarnation **we are free to create our own karmic fate by the choices we make daily, but we**

are always teleologically driven to realize our destined purpose which is to realize our divine nature—a fully realized Soul self; but life being what it is, our karmic fate may be at such variance with our destined purpose that *the omniscient guiding principle of life* (the "I Am" consciousness of God) has to intercede to put us right—as it did me when I was serendipitously introduced to Gurdjieff's teaching and Frank McMillan was serendipitously introduced to Carl Jung. This is the basic theme of Hopcke's *Synchronicity and the Stories of Our Lives*. "We receive in a synchronistic event a reminder of an important truth: that our lives are organized, consciously and unconsciously, the way a story is, that our lives have a coherence, a direction, a reason for being, and a beauty as well. Synchronicity reminds us how much a work of art the stories of our lives can be," writes Robert H. Hopcke.

As simply as I can possible put it then, experience has proven time and again that this *omniscient guiding principle of life*—and it doesn't matter what we call it—is always there to help us reconcile our karmic fate with our destined purpose, and happy are we when we comply with this benevolent guiding principle because our life runs much more smoothly.

But if we happen to be stubborn, as I was many times in my life (and in some of my past lives as well, as my seven past-life regressions have proven), we will be dragged yelling and screaming by our destined purpose until we are so desperate that we cry to God for help, as I did on the breakwater on the Nipigon River that day when I pleaded with God to help me find my way and was "inspired" to create my *Royal Dictum* which opened me up to the secret way in Gurdjieff's teaching, and just as I pleaded again with God when I experienced the incredible coincidence that I can now relate because this synchronistic event not only confirmed my belief in a benevolent guiding agency that is always here to assist us, but it also quickened my destined purpose by placing me in an ideal geographical location where I could become the writer I always wanted to be—here on the shores of Georgian Bay, South Central Ontario where Penny and I built our new home when we were "compelled" to leave my hometown of Nipigon for reasons which allowed for the symbolic manifestation of this incredible coincidence that I'm going to share in the following chapter…

16. A STREET CALLED STOCCO CIRCLE

"I know. I don't need to believe; I know..."

I am rounding the corner, and I can feel my story coming to closure with this and my next chapter; so if I may, let me offer by way of summation my gnostic but humble perspective on *the merciful law of divine synchronicity* before I relate what I consider to be proof positive (for me, anyway; but which may still not be enough to convince a sceptical reader) of an *omniscient guiding principle* in our daily life.

I make no claim to any special knowledge other than my own life-experience, which ironically initiated me into the sacred knowledge of the secret way that is open to everyone (if one has eyes to see and ears to hear, as Jesus would say), so what I have to say about the synchronicity principle would be purely subjective; but being subjective doesn't necessarily negate the objective reality of my life-experience, however incredible it may seem to be, and in the end it's left for the reader to decide on the credibility of my story.

But as I like to say, after years of studying the human condition through my own relationships with people and a lifetime of voracious reading and creative exploration through writing, it's always our choice as to what to believe, so why not believe in a perspective that embraces all beliefs, both the *being* and *non-being* aspects of human nature?

This is the deep mystery of synchronicity that opens the door for self-reconciliation, if we dare to risk it—as I did, for example, when I risked my university degree to take Gurdjieff's teaching out into the marketplace to forge my own path in life. And if I may, that's also how I got into business for myself when *the merciful law of divine synchronicity* opened a door for me to step out of one life path and into another that would eventually take me to university where serendipity introduced me to Gurdjieff's teaching which initiated me into the secret way of life that satisfied the desperate longing in my soul for wholeness.

Here's what happened: I was nineteen years old and working in a bush camp at the time when serendipity came calling (*serendipity has come calling many times in my life*). It was Saturday noon and a friend and I were standing outside the Nipigon Pool Hall on Front Street waiting for it to open, which it usually did at twelve o'clock every day; but it was getting on and still it hadn't opened, and we looked inside the window and saw the owner sweeping and cleaning from the previous day's business, but she didn't look very happy.

She saw us looking through the window and opened the door to explain that there was no-one to open the pool hall that day, and she was in tears at how the young man she had hired had left the place so messy. Why, I don't know; but I said to her that I would finish cleaning up and run the pool hall for her that day, and before I knew it I quit my job in the bush camp and got into the pool hall business.

I paid the elderly recently widowed Mrs. Atwill rent each month, and whatever I made was mine to keep; and in less than a month I had installed two pinball machines on consignment which made enough money to pay my rent every month with plenty left over. And a month or so later I installed another pin ball machine and a juke box on consignment, plus three cigarette vending machines that I placed elsewhere on consignment, one in *Leblanc's Restaurant* on Main Street, one in the *Nipigon Café,* and one in the *Husky Restaurant* on the highway, and I was headed for material success in the world of business.

But—*and here again we have another incredible BUT that will be sure to shock the psyche of the most skeptical reader*—this business path was not right for me to fulfill my destined purpose, and *the omniscient guiding principle of life* interceded and I divested myself of my pool hall and vending machine business after two years and went to Annecy, France to begin my quest for my true self because the path I was on was feeding my *non-being* and I had to get onto a path that would feed my *being* so I could *become* my true self—which Gurdjieff's teaching of "work on oneself" helped me to do after I returned from France and went to Lakehead University to study philosophy where I found Gurdjieff.

It seems like a long and circuitous route to get from point A to point B—from my pool hall and vending machine business to university where serendipity introduced me to Gurdjieff's teaching;

THE MERCIFUL LAW OF DIVINE SYNCHRONICITY

but this is the impenetrable mystery of *the omniscient guiding principle of life* that over time I came to simple call "Divine Spirit." And given all of the meaningful coincidences (*too many to remember*) that I had before and since I found my true self, all of which went a long way to keeping my karmic fate reconciled with my destined purpose, I came to the inevitable conclusion that our life is *providentially choreographed*—but always in keeping with our free will, which is the deepest secret of the synchronicity principle.

How can this be? How can we have free will and a destined purpose? As I have proven to myself over and over again, we are free to create our own karmic fate, but **if our karmic fate pulls us too far away from our destined purpose life intervenes with an experience like a meaningful coincidence that pulls our karmic fate closer to our destined purpose of** *becoming* **what we are meant to be.** Which brings me to the incredible coincidence of finding a building lot for our new home in Bluewater, Georgian Bay in South Central Ontario on a street—*believe it or not!* —named after me, STOCCO CIRCLE.

My name is Orest Stocco, but I was given a nickname when I operated the pool hall business in my hometown of Nipigon. My nickname was "Big O," which I got while playing in a pool tournament that I had put on to drum up business. Over time however, my nickname was reduced to simply "O." With an ironic smile, I like to say that this happened because life humbled me enough to take the "Big" out of my nickname and left me with just "O," which symbolizes zero; very humbling, indeed. But "O" is also a circle, as in STOCCO CIRCLE! (This speaks to what is known as the "Trickster," the playful side of synchronicity.)

But life will do that to us if we become overinflated with our own relevance, and I've seen this happen to many, many people; my favourite story being the humbling of the newspaper baron Lord Conrad Black, whose column I follow weekly in the paper that he founded and later sold, *The National Post*.

Conrad Moffat Black, Baron Black of Crossharbour, KSG is a Canadian-born British former newspaper publisher and author. He is a non-affiliated life peer. Black controlled Hollinger International, once the world's third-largest English-language newspaper empire, which published *The Daily Telegram, Chicago Sun-Times, The Jerusalem*

Post, National Post, and hundreds of community newspapers in North America, before he was fired by the board of Hollinger in 2004.

Lord Black was at the pinnacle of his career when his life came crashing down. He was charged for fraud and obstruction of justice (to this day he claims his innocence) and served time in an American prison; but what fascinated me about this extraordinary man was not his gargantuan ego, intimidating intelligence (he's also a historian and author of several biographies and history books and personal memoirs (whose vocabulary always sends me to the dictionary), and entrepreneurial genius, but his *daemonic* drive to get the most and best out of life. To make the point, this is what he said about his brilliant and beautiful wife, the journalist Barbara Amiel whose memoir *Confessions* I read years ago and whose column I have followed in *Maclean's* magazine: "She is the epitome of my most ardent desire."

Unlike so many highly successful and accomplished people who fall from grace and cannot redeem themselves (they usually become bitter and angry at life), Lord Black had a *metanoic* change of heart after his public humiliation, which I observed over the years in his weekly column in the *National Post;* and I admire and respect him for his unbreakable spirit which the poet William Earnest Henley so beautifully captured in his poem *Invictus:*

> Out of the night that covers me,
>   Black as the Pit from pole to pole,
> I thank whatever gods may be
>   For my unconquerable soul.
>
> In the fell clutch of circumstance
>   I have not winced nor cried aloud,
> Under the bludgeoning of chance
>   My head is bloody, but unbowed.
>
> Beyond this place of wrath and tears
>   Looms but the horror of the shade,
> And yet the menace of the years
>   Finds, and shall find me, unafraid.

THE MERCIFUL LAW OF DIVINE SYNCHRONICITY

> It matters not how straight the gate,
> How charged with punishment the scroll,
> I am the master of my fate:
> I am the captain of my soul.

Lord Conrad Black's *metanoic* change of heart illustrates what I have come to recognize as *the corrective principle of life* that brings one's karmic fate back into alignment with one's destined purpose when it has strayed too far from the telos of life, which is the realization of our true self; and as cruel as *the corrective principle of life* may appear to be, as in Lord Black's fall from grace and devastating public humiliation (his "friends" abandoned him like rats a sinking ship), it is always for our own good; and if we have the wisdom to see it, we thank God for the experience—as some people do who get cancer and thank God for their life-changing experience, like Jungian analyst Marion Woodman.

Marion Woodman recorded her cancer experience in her courageous and inspiring book *Bone: A Journal of Wisdom, Strength, and Healing*. In the Forward, she writes: "Cancer has made me sadder and wiser, and therefore richer. Because death is an essential part of life, to be fully alive is to be prepared for it. Cancer has prepared me. And that makes me grateful for my life, present to it and in it to a degree that life before cancer never attained. The gift of cancer is the gift of Now, a sense of all time precariously lodged within it. Living with death is a more abundant life." And she ends her Forward with the following words, which sum up the theme of this book on *the merciful law of divine synchronicity* in a way that only someone who has passed through the eye of the needle possibly could: **"Fate is the death we owe to Nature. Destiny is the life we owe to soul."**

Marion Woodman's life-transforming experience, plus dozens and dozens of other stories that I have read of life-transforming experiences brought about by *the corrective principle of life*—not to mention my own harrowing experience of life grabbing me by the scruff of the neck and bringing me back kicking and screaming to my destined purpose—these stories have all brought me to the simple realization that **there is an all-knowing benevolent guiding principle in life that serves our destined purpose of realizing our**

true self; and it doesn't matter how much pain and suffering we have to go through because of our recalcitrant spirit (regardless how many lifetimes we have to live), we will all become what we are meant to be—*because this is our destined purpose!*

Now I can relate the incredible coincidence that landed me on a street synchronistically named after me in Tiny Township, Georgian Bay Ontario ...

This incredible coincidence was initiated fifteen years ago. (As I said, synchronicities don't just happen; they presuppose their own history.) I was getting on in years, and I began to feel an ominous sense of dread that I would never get to tell my remarkable story of self-discovery because, after all, who knew when I would shuffle off my mortal coil?

That was the inception of my incredible coincidence, because my dread of dying without telling my story kicked in *the merciful law of divine synchronicity* (it's not unusual for synchronicities to happen when one is in deep emotional turmoil) which opened the door for me to reconcile my karmic fate with my destined purpose; but I did not know this at the time. I just went with the experience as it was happening to me.

One evening I was perusing my monthly QPB book club selections that had just come in the mail when I came across Ruth Picardie's *Before I Say Goodbye,* the true story of her reflections in the final year of her cancer-stricken life, and as I wrote in my own book which Picardie's book inspired, "in one sudden burst of creative awareness my life flashed before my eyes, and I knew what I had to do"—*which was to tell the story of my own life!* That's how I got to write my first self-published novel that upset my hometown so much that my life partner Penny Lynn and I had to relocate to Bluewater, Georgian Bay for peace of mind.

But this was not without precedent. Many writers have written stories that have upset their own community, like Alice Munroe who when asked by Shelagh Rogers on CBC's radio show *Morningside* what the people of her hometown thought of her stories, she replied: "I don't know. They don't speak to me." Until, that is, she became one of Canada's best writers with an international reputation who went on to win the Nobel Prize in Literature in 2013; now her home

THE MERCIFUL LAW OF DIVINE SYNCHRONICITY

town not only remembers her, but prides itself on its most famous citizen.

My favorite story of a community's disenchantment with a writer however is Thomas Wolfe's publication of the novel that launched his career, *Look Homeward, Angel*. This novel so upset his hometown of Asheville, North Carolina that he was reviled for his portrayal of the people of Asheville—just as I was reviled for how I portrayed the people of my hometown of Nipigon, Northwestern Ontario in my autobiographical novel *What Would I Say Today If I Were to Die Tomorrow?*

Actually, I wrote two autobiographical novels in the same year that were self-published and launched simultaneously in the Nipigon Arena in my hometown on a long weekend. The other was *On the Wings of Habitat,* which was inspired by my experience volunteering my time and skills (I had my own drywall taping and painting business) for Habitat for Humanity in Thunder Bay, which I did for five summers; so I was doubly cursed, because *On the Wings of Habitat* further added to the threat that *What Would I Say Today If I Were to Die Tomorrow?* had upon the shadow personality of my hometown that my novels brought to light (*as I learned at a dear cost, readers love to read about the shadow side of another person's personality, but not their own*); and so vitriolic was the hatred for myself and my life partner that Penny and I decided to relocate to Georgian Bay.

How this came about is a story in itself, which I plan to write one day when I'm called upon to write it (I can hear the faint whisper of my Muse in my ear, which means that within a year or so I'll be writing *We May Be Tiny, But We're Not Small*, an autobiographical novel inspired by our harrowing experience in my hometown of Nipigon, Ontario); so suffice for this story that when Penny and I drove to Wasaga Beach for a short leafing holiday the following month after the launching of my two novels, we decided to move to this part of Ontario, and when we got back home we made plans to put a mortgage on our triplex in Nipigon and build a new home in Tiny Township, Georgian Bay.

But it's how we found the building lot for our new home that speaks to *the merciful law of divine synchronicity,* because on the Saturday morning that I left to drive back down to Wasaga Beach to meet up with Penny's long-time friend who was going to drive me around to look for a building lot for our new home that his carpenter son was going to build for us, I hugged Penny to say goodbye and she said to me, "Please find us a nice lot for our new home," and with tears in my eyes I kissed my love and left for my long drive.

I wasn't going down blind however, because Penny and I had done research for building lots on the Internet, and we had selected four or five prospects, starting in the town of Meaford, then Thornbury, and then Wasaga Beach; but there was so much pressure on me to find the right building lot for our new home that I turned to God for help.

"God," I said, *"my back is to the wall, and I need help. Please give me a sign which lot to buy. But I don't want just any sign. Give me an unequivocal sign or none at all."*

When I got to Wasaga Beach Sunday afternoon (it's a long drive and I stayed overnight in Sault Ste. Marie), I got a motel room and looked up Penny's friend, and Monday morning we went looking for the right building lot for our new home.

We drove to Meaford first, but the two prospects did not feel right, and we looked in Thornbury and Wasaga Beach, but they just did not speak to me; and then Penny's friend said that a contractor friend of his had told him that there were building lots down in Tiny Beaches, so we drove down into what felt like the boondocks to me, and I cannot express how much stress I felt as we drove down Country Road 29 to where these lots were to be found. It was my last hope, and it felt like the longest drive of my life!

I had no idea of course that this was prime Georgian Bay cottage country because I did not know the area, so when we finally came to the intersection of Country Road 29 and Tiny Beaches Road I felt some relief because as we drove down Tiny Beaches Road I saw that there was a whole subdivision of nice homes, and we drove around the subdivision looking for real estate signs on empty lots. We drove around for ten minutes or so, and then we came upon a street called STOCCO CIRCLE and my heart stopped!

I couldn't believe my eyes. Barry stopped the truck and I got out to look at the street sign up close and then pleaded with God, *"Please let there be a lot for sale here."* And as *the merciful law of divine synchronicity* would have it, there was only one lot for sale on

THE MERCIFUL LAW OF DIVINE SYNCHRONICITY

STOCCO CIRCLE, and as we later found out it had just gone up for sale on the Saturday morning that I drove down to Wasaga Beach and I was the first person to put a bid on it!

The owner was asking thirty-five thousand, five thousand below the forty thousand budget that we had allotted for a lot, and I bid thirty-four and he came back at thirty-four five, and I bought it (*within the next two to three years the secret was out, and the building lots doubled in price!*); and the following spring Barry's son Brian and his partner began building our new home in Georgian Bay, and fourteen years into our new home and we couldn't have asked for a better location to begin our new life in Bluewater, Tiny Beaches!

"Of all the areas that we've seen down here," Penny said to me three or four years after we moved into our new home, "I like our area best." Silently, I thanked God for finding us the perfect building lot for our new home and our new life which afforded me the work I needed for my trade because of all the building going on in the area, and for the time and solitude for all the writing that I would be doing after my open-heart surgery; but that's a story that I'm reserving for my novel *We May Be Tiny, But We're Not Small...*

17. THE VOICE WITHIN

"We must remember that nothing in this world is accidental, everything has its final purpose..."

Because I asked God for an unequivocal sign for the right building lot for our new home in Georgian Bay and got a literal/symbolic sign in the street sign STOCCO CIRCLE, I had to concede that this went beyond meaningful coincidence and fell into the province of divine intercession; this is how I came up with the concept of *the merciful law of divine synchronicity*, because in my desperate need I asked God for an unequivocal sign and got it!

In a way, this incredible coincidence was the icing on the cake of all the meaningful coincidences that I had experienced in my life, and I had experienced many; so it's not like I had abandoned to the concept of a merciful law of divine synchronicity; I had experienced the benevolence of the synchronistic principle before, but never like finding a street named after me which was so symbolically perfect that it had a remarkable healing effect upon my bruised psyche given the devastating effect that my two novels had upon my community, and I can understand why Thomas Wolfe would write a book called *You Can't Go Home Again* because it took me eleven years before I dared return to my hometown of Nipigon!

Can you imagine having a home on a street named after you if you are a writer hoping to make a success of your writing career? It's like God was telling me in that humorous way that has been attributed to the playful spirit of the synchronistic principle that it didn't matter if my hometown didn't appreciate my writing, the Universe did and rewarded me by placing me on a street named after me! How many writers can claim such distinction despite not having achieved a level of recognition that would honour them with a street named after them? *The irony of this incredible coincidence is beyond comprehension!*

"An experience of synchronicity is a soul moment," said Phil Cousineau in his book *Soul Moments*, if I may be allowed to quote him again, "an electrifying experience, a sudden visitation by a god, a palpable inrush of grace and power, one of the defining moments in life, a sudden conviction that we might move beyond fate and realize a hint of our destiny"—which is exactly what I experienced when I found a building lot for our new home on STOCCO CIRCLE in Bluewater, Tiny Beaches because this symbol spoke to my destined purpose of becoming the writer I always wanted to be, and in the fourteen years that we have been here I've written and published more than twenty books with more to come, and maybe one day I will be acknowledged enough to dignify living on a street named after me.

Now, on to the resolution of my story...

If asked if I believe in God, I would reply as Carl Jung replied to John Freeman in the now-famous BBC interview if he believed in God and Jung replied, *"I know. I don't need to believe, I know,"* and I *know* because for me God is not a concept or archetypal image (which he may very well be besides being what I believe God to be, the foundation of all things), and I came to this realization not simply because of all the books that I have read and studied, and not because of the various spiritual paths that I have lived (*I haven't even mentioned an offshoot Christian solar cult teaching that I'm reserving for a novel, if I ever find the courage to write it because this solar teaching did irreparable damage to my eyesight!*), but because of personal experience that has given me a gnostic certainty that God exists; and aside from looking into the Face of God (the most ineffable experience of my life which I shouldn't even have mentioned because it opens me up to the ridicule of incredulity), one of these experiences was hearing the voice of what Emerson called "God within" but which I simply call my Higher Self because it sounds much less dramatic.

But dramatic or not, our Higher Self is our divine nature, and it took me many years to realize that the voice within that asked me *"Why do you lie?"* when I hit a brick wall with Gurdjieff's teaching of "work on oneself" was the voice of "God within" that is always present and ready to assist us in our desperate time of need, and believe me I was desperate; but that question was so powerful that it freed me from the hold my shadow had upon me!

Which brings me to a spiritual musing I wrote that was inspired by an experience my life partner Penny Lynn had one day while working her job as a Hallmark rep in the Walmart store in Wasaga Beach, an experience that confirmed the presence of *the omniscient guiding principle of life*, whether we call it God within or Higher Self, that is always there to help reconcile our karmic fate with our destined purpose, as it did with Penny Lynn's incredible experience that I explored in my spiritual musing:—

"Go to the Casino"
Reflections on the Voice Within

This is a dangerous musing, and I don't want to write it; but when my Muse whispers into my ear I have to do what I have been called to do, for such is the nature of the mysterious relationship between the writer and his inspiration.

The idea for today's spiritual musing has been gestating for years waiting for the right conditions to set it free, which came with an experience that my life partner Penny Lynn had this past summer when she went to work one day and heard a voice say to her, not once but three times, "Go to the casino," but I would never write this musing had she not given me permission to share her incredible experience.

But aside from Penny's experience, which gives today's musing on the voice within anecdotal credibility because I trust Penny Lynn implicitly, I have a precedent in my favorite philosopher Socrates whom Plato tells us in the *Apology* was guided all of his life by an inner voice that he called his "oracle."

"This is a sign I have had ever since I was a child," said Socrates at his trial in Athens for sedition and heresy. "The sign is a voice which comes to me and always forbids me to do something which I am going to do, but never commands me to do anything, and this is what stands in the way of my being a politician."

Socrates had inner guidance, as we all do; but not all of us hear an inner voice, and if we do, it speaks to us according to our needs and destined purpose as it did to Socrates and my life partner Penny Lynn. And I too heard an inner voice when I hit a brick wall with Gurdjieff's teaching of "work on oneself" and did not know where to turn; the voice within was loud and clear, and it said to me: *"Why do you lie?"*

This simple question was like a stick of dynamite that blew a hole in my life and set me free from my false self (which Gurdjieff called our "false personality" and Carl Jung called our "shadow," the unconscious side of our ego personality), because the more I focused on what I said and did the more acutely conscious I became of my own falseness; and this simple question that came from within set me on the path to my true self which I wrote about forty years later in *The Summoning of Noman*.

So, the question that is crying to be asked today is this: what is this inner voice, this guidance that comes from within that said to Penny Lynn, "Go to the casino"?

Socrates, best known to the world for his famous words **"the unexamined life is not worth living,"** called his oracle "the divinity." And Eileen Caddy, one of the founding members (along with her husband Peter and Dorothy Maclean) of the New Age spiritual community of Findhorn in northern Scotland, which became renowned for its legendary garden of giant vegetables, called her guiding voice "the God within." She also referred to her inner guidance as "the still, small voice within." I call it my intuitive, or Higher Self; but why would this be a dangerous musing to write?

When Eileen Caddy first heard the voice within she had just written a letter to her husband Andrew Combe, who was stationed in Iraq, asking him for a divorce; and he replied immediately, forbidding her to see their five children. It was at this time that a traumatized Eileen visited a private sanctuary in Glastonbury with her future husband Peter Caddy where while meditating she heard the voice within say to her, "Be still and know that I am God." She thought she was having a nervous breakdown, but over time she began "to love the voice as an instrument from the God within us all," and she continued to be guided by the voice within which helped her to found the spiritual community of Findhorn that went on to become a beacon of light for the world; and I can't help but feel that this is a dangerous musing because in this materialist world of ours anyone who talks about hearing the voice of God will be sure to invite ridicule, which is why I refer to the voice within as our intuitive, or Higher Self. But I didn't come to this insight lightly. As a matter of fact, it took many years of anguished living before I made the connection...

We all have hunches, nudges, gut feelings, and compulsions to do things— *"I just feel I have to do this,"* we say when we're caught in the grips of our destined purpose; and more often than not, the course of our life is changed. But why did we feel compelled to do what we did, like my compulsion to take up Gurdjieff's teaching?

Without going into detail, which I've done in *The Summoning of Noman*, in my quest for my true self I had seven past-life regressions; and in one of my regressions I was miraculously brought back to the Body of God where all new souls come from, but I had no individual self-consciousness. I was an atom of God in the Body of God, and I had consciousness but no self-consciousness; and in the same regression I went back to my first primordial human lifetime on earth as a higher primate where I experienced the dawning of my reflective self-consciousness, and with each successive incarnation I grew in the consciousness of my reflective self through the natural process of karma and reincarnation until in my current lifetime I felt compelled to take evolution into my own hands with Gurdjieff's teaching and realize my true self, which I've written about in *The Pearl of Great Price* that was inspired by Christ's most sacred parable.

I discovered reincarnation in my teens, and in my long journey of self-discovery I came to see that we all have two destinies—one personal, which is born of our will to choose freely, and one spiritual, which is pre-scripted by our divine nature; and our purpose in life is to grow in our personal destiny until we are evolved enough to align our personal destiny with our spiritual destiny and realize our true self, which Jesus called "the pearl of great price."

"Again, the kingdom of heaven is like a merchant seeking beautiful pearls. Who, when he had found one pearl of great price, went and sold all that he had and bought it," said Jesus in coded language for the call to one's true self; and it is this call to one's destined purpose that I refer to as the "omniscient guiding principle of life" which is the voice within that speaks to us in our moments of need and destined purpose, as it did to Socrates, Eileen Caddy, my life partner, and myself and every person in the world though few people make the connection because it implies that we're all divine beings in the process of becoming one with God which is too much for people to deal with. But then, didn't Jesus say, *"I and my Father are one"?*

"There is a doctrine uttered in secret that man is a prisoner who has no right to open the door of his prison and run away," said Socrates in Plato's *Phaedo*. "This is a great mystery which I do not quite understand. Yet I, too, believe that the gods are our guardians, and that we are a possession of theirs," added Socrates, again speaking in the coded language of the secret way that we are imprisoned in the eternal cycle of life and death and the purpose of life is to grow in our own identity through karma and reincarnation until nature can evolve us no further and we have to complete what nature cannot finish by taking evolution into our own hands to realize our true self, which Gurdjieff's teaching helps one to do—and Christ's teaching, along with other teachings like Sufism and Taoism, and always aided by the omniscient guiding principle of life that speaks to us as the voice within.

This implies a benevolent intelligence that watches over us, which over time I had no choice but to believe because of the many synchronicities in my life that always assisted me in my times of desperate need, so when Penny heard the voice say to her "Go to the casino" not once but three times, each time after her objection because she could not justify taking time off work to go to the casino, which speaks to her character, I had to ask myself—knowing what I do about the omniscient guiding principle of life that is forever working on our behalf to help bring our personal destiny into agreement with our spiritual destiny—why did the voice want Penny to take time off work to go to the casino? What divine purpose was there in going to the casino?

I had no idea, and the other morning over coffee in my writing room I asked her to relate the whole experience which I recorded on my mini-recorder that I used when I taped my ten sessions with the psychic medium who channeled St. Padre Pio which became the basis of my novel *Healing with Padre Pio*, and with Penny's permission, I'm going to include the entire transcript of her incredible casino experience: —

O: So, what happened that day?

PL: I was working at Walmart, or I was going to work at Walmart—

O: You heard the voice before you went to work?

PL: I was sitting in my car. I had a Tcheck'it call to do at Walmart, and I had just arrived at Walmart. I was sitting in my car because my Tcheck'it app kept asking me for my location. The application has a GPS on it, so when you go from town to town it picks up your location so it can give you driving directions to the store. For some odd reason, when I left home that morning I knew there were calls at Walmart in Wasaga Beach, because the application notifies you by text message when there are calls in your area, and I had signed up for this Tcheck'it through MCA (Merchandizing Consultants Association). They thought it would be a way for reps to make a little extra money and a kind of a fun thing to do. So anyway, I had come from the Dollarama Store in the morning and was about to go in to do my call at Walmart for Hallmark, and with

THE MERCIFUL LAW OF DIVINE SYNCHRONICITY

Tcheck'it you always have to take a picture of the outside of the store that you're at just to verify that you were at that store, and I thought I would take my picture as I was going into the store first before doing my Tcheck'it call so I wouldn't have to do it after I took the rest of my pictures in the store and answer the questions for my call. Well anyway the GPS wouldn't pick up my location, and for some odd reason it wouldn't load the call; so I'm sitting in the car having my coffee and I'm trying to get my location sorted out on the Tcheck'it app and I hear this voice, and it says to me, "Go to the casino." Just as plain as day, "Go to the casino"—

O: You heard this voice in your head?

PL: No. I heard it out loud. It said, "Go to the casino." I don't know if it was in my head or whatever, but I mean it was like someone was sitting there talking—

O: And it said, "Go to the casino"?

PL: It said, "Go to the casino." And I said no, I can't go to the casino. I'm working. But the thing is, the day was August 13th. It was the 29th anniversary of my brother's death—

O: And you were very close to your brother—

PL: I was very, very close to my brother, and I felt that was like a guiding voice from him, or after the fact I thought, I wasn't really sure; I didn't really think of it at that particular time; but anyway, I just said no, I can't go to the casino, I'm working. So anyway, I'm sitting there—

O: Did it sound like your brother's voice though?

PL: It was just a male voice. No, it didn't sound specifically like his voice. It was just a voice—

O: A male voice?

PL: Well, you know; it's really even hard to say whether the voice had a gender. It was a directional voice. That's the only way I can describe it. For me, it was; it sounded more on the male side. So then, I'm sitting in my car having my coffee and trying to get my application to work, and for the second time I hear this voice talk to me, and it said, "Go to the casino," and once again I answered, no, I'm not going to the casino, I'm working. Anyway, about twenty minutes had gone by and I'm still fiddling with the application on my phone—

O: Why are you fiddling?

PL: I'm trying to get it to load the location so that the calls would come up. None of the calls were coming up, because for some odd reason the GPS wasn't picking up my location, and without the location the APP can't determine whether there's calls in your area. So anyway, after fiddling with that for about twenty minutes I said to myself, you know, for a three-dollar call, is it worth all of this aggravation? And at that point I heard that voice for the third time, and it said, "*Go* to the casino." So I said, okay, alright; first of all, though, I have to go into Walmart, go to the washroom, and I have to stop at the bank and deposit a cheque, and I will go to the casino. And that's what I did.

O: Okay, you went to the casino?

PL: I went to the casino, and I wasn't there very long—

O: The casino is the Georgian Downs casino?

PL: Georgian Downs in Innisfil, just outside Barrie.

O: About an hour's drive?

PL: No, about forty minutes. But the thing is, I kind of felt a little bit guilty because I always call you at lunch time, and it was getting pretty close to lunchtime. Actually, it was lunchtime just as I was pulling into Georgian Downs, and I had to tell you a little fib because I didn't want to say that I listened to this little voice in my head and went to the casino; and, it's not something that I would normally do. I don't normally go somewhere without telling you; but I was compelled by this voice to follow this through. So I thought, well, for now I'm not going to say anything. I can always fess up later. Anyway, I made my call to you, and I got into the casino, and I'm not there very long, and I win money. And I kept winning money. And I had actually won over eleven hundred dollars, but it was too early to come home and I told you I was at work, and I thought if I drive home now you're going to think, well holy molly, that was really a short day; so I decided to stay there and play a little bit more. I mean, I did play down almost two hundred dollars of what I had won, but it was fine; and I came out of there with nine hundred and fifteen dollars.

O: And that's it? You didn't hear the voice anymore?

PL: Never heard the voice anymore, never heard the voice since.

That was Penny's casino experience. But because she heard the voice within once before when we were going through troubled waters in our relationship because of my regressions which brought back the memory of our past lifetime together in Genoa, Italy when we were man and wife and I betrayed our family honor by humiliating my wife on the dance floor with my mistress at the biggest social event of the year, I broke my wife's heart and she never spoke to me again. That's why we got together in this lifetime; I had to mend her broken heart, which made our relationship much more than the eye could see, because when I went back to that lifetime in my regression all hell broke loose and Penny was ready to pack her bags and leave me. But on a walk one evening she heard the voice within, and she decided to stay; but because this is so personal I'm not going to reveal what the voice said to her, and I mention this only to verify the point I want to make with today's spiritual musing.

Had I not had my seven past-life regressions, I would never have connected the dots and discerned our purpose in life; but because I did, I know from personal experience that we come from the Body of God to grow and evolve through life until nature has evolved us enough to give birth to a new "I" of God, as I experienced, and from lifetime to lifetime we continue to grow in the "I" of God (our own reflective self-consciousness) until nature can evolve us no further through karma and reincarnation and we have to complete what nature cannot finish by taking evolution into our own hands, as I did with Gurdjieff's teaching. We are all atoms of God's Body, and God watches over us every moment of the day, and whenever we need guidance to bring our personal destiny into agreement with our spiritual destiny God speaks to us, as it did to Penny Lynn.

But what did her going to the casino have to do with bringing her personal destiny into agreement with her spiritual destiny? That's the mystery of the voice within, and the point of today's spiritual musing...

From the moment an atom of God gives birth to a new "I" of God, it separates from the evolving collective consciousness of life and creates its own personal destiny out of its encoded purpose to grow in the "I" of God; and when the atom of God has grown enough in its own identity to realize that life can do no more to satisfy its longing to become all that it is meant to be, the atom of God must find a way to satisfy this longing; but how? Where does it look to satisfy this longing?

"As each plant grows from a seed and becomes in the end an oak tree, so man must become what he is meant to be. He ought to get there, but most get stuck," said Jung; and, sad to say, we all get stuck in one lifetime or another and in anger shout a variation of Macbeth's lament that "life is a tale told by an idiot full of sound and fury signifying nothing." But nothing could be further from the truth, and whether it happens in this lifetime or the next the divine logic of life will bring our personal destiny into agreement with our spiritual destiny to fulfill our destined purpose; and after much reflection I finally reasoned out the logic of Penny's casino experience.

The reason we get stuck on our destined journey to our true self is because we have created a karmic pattern that will not allow us to transcend ourselves, and Penny had created a karmic pattern in her attitude towards money that inhibited her spiritual growth; and no matter what she did, she could not break this mental habit. That's why providence intervened with the voice within by telling her to go to the casino.

The only reason Penny listened to the voice within and went to the casino was because she finally realized that all of her aggravation to do her Tcheck'it call wasn't worth the three dollars she would be getting. It wasn't going to change her financial situation, and she threw her hands into the air and said, "Alright, I'll go to the casino if that's what you want me to do." And she went and came home with $915.00 which paid for our little trip up north to visit her family the following month.

Penny's casino experience broke her karmic pattern of worrying over money, because it inhibited her spiritual growth; but because she could not break this karmic pattern on her own, divine providence intervened.

That's why we hear the voice within, to help us get unstuck and bring our personal destiny into agreement with our spiritual destiny so we can continue on our destined journey to wholeness and completeness. And whether we call the voice within God or Higher Self, it does not matter; it is our personal oracle and guiding principle, and it is always there to assist us in times of need.

———

Full disclosure. Penny heard the voice within two more times nine months later, each time saying the same thing: "Go to the casino." The second time she was told to go to the casino, she won $3,785.00; and the next time a week later she won $3,004.00; and to add icing to the cake, the voice spoke to her once again several months later on *January 30, 2017,* and she came home with $3,768.30.

Good luck, or divine intervention? As William Shatner liked to say on his TV show on strange experiences, *"weird or what?"* But I firmly believe that Penny Lynn was told to go to the casino three more times to fix the new pattern in her mind and stop worrying about money and get on with her destined purpose of becoming her true self; and, believe me, it's a joy watching her unfolding uninhibited by that old worrisome karmic pattern because the more she *becomes* her true self, the more she brings to our relationship.

"*As each plant grows from a seed and becomes in the end an oak tree, so man must become what he is meant to be. He ought to get there, but most get stuck,*" said Jung, and it is my firm conviction that whenever we get stuck on the way to our destined purpose, *the omniscient guiding principle of life* will be there to help us get unstuck, as it helped Penny Lynn break that karmic pattern that inhibited her spiritual growth and as it helped me get unstuck many times in my long journey of self-discovery, and as it helps every soul find their way out of the karmic patterns that keep them from realizing their destined purpose.

And with this, I can bring my story on *the merciful law of divine synchronicity* to resolution; because to say any more would only be redundant. We are all born to become what we are meant to be, and we will all get there eventually; whether in this lifetime or the next, it does not matter, because in God's time there is no end to our *becoming*.

*****

About the Author

Born with a spiritual restlessness that could not be tamed by my Christian faith, I became a spiritual seeker when I discovered reincarnation in Plato's Dialogues at the age of fifteen. I grew up in a small town in Northwestern Ontario, and at twenty-one I had my own pool hall and vending machine business, but my restless spirit called me away to seek out my destiny, and I sold my business and sailed to France.

In the Alpine city of Annecy, in the Haute-Savoie region of France I had a dream that called me to my destiny. I entered into the mind of every person in the world and took every question they had ever asked and reduced them all to one question: *Why am I?* I returned to Canada and went to university to study philosophy to seek an answer to this haunting question, and by "chance" I discovered Gurdjieff, the redoubtable teacher of a system of transformative thought that he called "the Work." His Teaching excited my restless spirit and compelled me to seek out the answer to man's disquieting question in the fast, often tumultuous currents of daily living.

Visit him at: http://ostocco.wix.com/ostocco
Spiritual Musings Blog:
http://www.spiritualmusingsbyoreststocco.blogspot.com

ALSO BY OREST STOCCO

NOVELS

The Golden Seed
Tea with Grace
Jesus Wears Dockers
Healing with Padre Pio
Keeper of the Flame
My Unborn Child
On the Wings of Habitat
What Would I Say Today If I Were to Die Tomorrow?

NON-FICTION

Death, the Final Frontier
Gurdjieff was wrong but his teaching works…
The Man of God Walks Alone
The Summoning of Noman
The Lion that Swallowed Hemingway
The Sum of All Spiritual Paths
Do We Have An Immortal Soul?
Stupidity Is Not a Gift of God
Letters to Padre Pio
Old Whore Life
Just Going with the Flow
Why Bother? The Riddle of the Good Samaritan
The Pearl of Great Price
In The Shade of the Maple Tree

www.ingramcontent.com/pod-product-compliance
Lightning Source LLC
LaVergne TN
LVHW011420080426
835512LV00005B/172